M366 Block 1
UNDERGRADUATE COMPUTING

Natural and
artificial intelligence

Intelligent machines

Block 1

Cover image: Daniel H. Janzen. *Polistes* wasps build a relatively simple nest that lasts only a single summer. These New World wasps often site the unenclosed combs under eaves and the other sheltered places where they come into contact with people.

This publication forms part of an Open University course M366 *Natural and artificial intelligence.* Details of this and other Open University courses can be obtained from the Student Registration and Enquiry Service, The Open University, PO Box 197, Milton Keynes MK7 6BJ, United Kingdom: tel. +44 (0)845 300 6090, email general-enquiries@open.ac.uk

Alternatively, you may visit the Open University website at http://www.open.ac.uk where you can learn more about the wide range of courses and packs offered at all levels by The Open University.

To purchase a selection of Open University course materials visit http://www.ouw.co.uk, or contact Open University Worldwide, Michael Young Building, Walton Hall, Milton Keynes MK7 6AA, United Kingdom for a brochure. tel. +44 (0)1908 858793; fax +44 (0)1908 858787; email ouw-customer-services@open.ac.uk

The Open University
Walton Hall, Milton Keynes
MK7 6AA

First published 2007

Edited, designed and typeset by The Open University.

Printed and bound in the United Kingdom by The Charlesworth Group, Wakefield.

ISBN 978 0 7492 1578 1

1.1

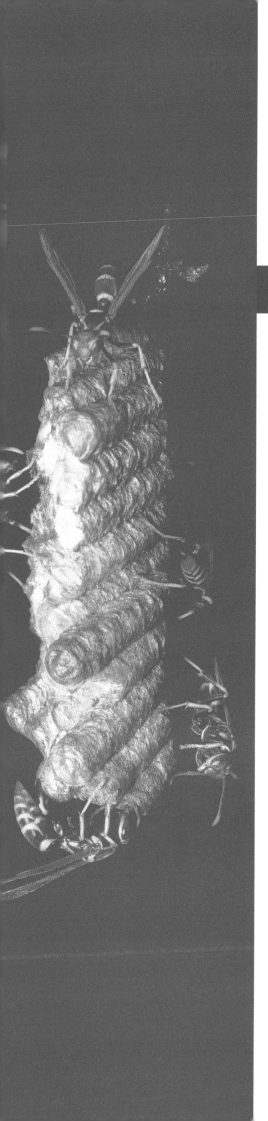

Block 1
Intelligent machines

Prepared for the Course Team by Chris Dobbyn

CONTENTS

M366 COURSE TEAM

Chair, author and academic editor
Chris Dobbyn

Authors
Mustafa Ali

Tony Hirst

Mike Richards

Neil Smith

Patrick Wong

External assessor
Nigel Crook, Oxford Brookes University

Course managers
Gaynor Arrowsmith

Linda Landsberg

Media development staff
Andrew Seddon, Media Project Manager

Garry Hammond, Editor

Kate Gentles, Freelance Editor

Callum Lester, Software Developer

Andrew Whitehead, Designer and Graphic Artist

Phillip Howe, Compositor

Sarah Gamman, Contracts Executive

Lydia Eaton, Media Assistant

Critical readers
Frances Chetwynd

John Dyke

Ian Kenny

Paolo Remagnino

Thanks are due to the Desktop Publishing Unit of the Faculty of Mathematics and Computing.

Introduction to Block 1

Block introduction

The idea of building intelligent machines with mental capacities comparable to, or better than, those of human beings seems to have been an endlessly fascinating one. By the middle of the 20th century, hopes were running high that such a goal might really be achieved. *Artificial intelligence* (AI) would be the key.

Joseph Weizenbaum, of the Massachusetts Institute of Technology's AI Laboratory, suggested that the objective was:

> nothing less than to build a machine on the model of man, a robot that is to have its childhood, to learn language as a child does, to gain its knowledge of the world by sensing the world through its own organs, and ultimately to contemplate the whole domain of human thought.

Others went even further. Edward Fredkin, also of MIT's AI Lab, suggested in a BBC 'Horizon' programme of 1983 that such machines could become super-intelligent and 'may condescend to talk to us, ... and ... they may keep us as pets'.

How realistic is such a prospect? And is this really the goal of artificial intelligence? What steps have been taken towards this goal, and what is the thinking that underlies such wild claims? These are some of the questions I want to raise and try to tackle in this block.

Block 1 contains just one unit.

Unit 1: Machines, minds and computers

This unit sets out to review, briefly, the development of human thinking about machines and our own mental abilities, and how the digital computer came about. The material is both historical and technical, and leads up to the Cybernetics and Symbolic AI movements in the late 20th century.

Block 1 learning outcomes

After studying this block you will be able to:

▶ write a brief explanation of the aims of, and motivations for, artificial intelligence;

▶ identify, and briefly outline, the ideas of some key thinkers about mind and intelligence;

▶ write a paragraph discussing the meaning of the term 'intelligence' and various possible tests for intelligence in humans and machines;

▶ explain the basic principles of the digital computer and its role in artificial intelligence;

▶ compare and contrast the projects of Symbolic AI and Cybernetics.

Unit 1: Machines, minds and computers

CONTENTS

Introduction to Unit 1

The real question is not whether machines think but whether men do.

Source: B. F. Skinner, *Contingencies of Reinforcement* (1969)

In this unit I want to offer you a panoramic view of the intellectual background to the ideas we're going to cover in this course. There are four principal sections – 'Machines', 'Minds', 'AI' and 'Computers' – framed by this introduction and some conclusions and reflections.

Briefly, this is the ground I want to cover:

▶   *Machines.* In this section we'll look at the history of humanity's engagement with machine technologies and at our dream of building machines that share our special human features and powers – particularly our mental abilities.

▶   *Minds.* Here, we'll explore the development of the idea that human thought might be a form of computation, from its origins in the 17th century, through the advent of the digital computer in the 20th, and into the Cybernetics and Symbolic AI movements of the recent past and the present.

▶   *AI.* In this section we'll examine the birth and intellectual foundations of Symbolic AI and contrast it with the Cybernetic approach. We will also look at the distinction between *strong* and *weak artificial intelligence*.

▶   *Computers.* Almost all of us have some experience of working with computers. Most of us probably feel confident we know what they are, and what they can do. In this section we'll examine the fundamental concept of the digital computer as an *interpreted automatic formal system* and consider the implications of this for computational theories of mind.

At the end, I'll try to draw some conclusions and set the scene for the course ahead. Some of the material in the unit is historical, some technical – all of it is relevant to the theme of M366: humanity's quest to build intelligent machines.

What you need to study this unit

You will need the following course components, and will need to use your computer and internet connection for some of the exercises.

▶   this Block 1 text
▶   the course DVD.

LEARNING OUTCOMES FOR UNIT 1

After studying this unit you will be able to:

1.1 describe a number of artificial creatures, in myth, legend, fiction and fact;

1.2 write a paragraph describing the intellectual origins of the computational picture of mind;

1.3 explain the distinction drawn in this course between artificial intelligence and Symbolic AI;

1.4 write a short paragraph comparing and contrasting the key principles and strategies of Cybernetics and of Symbolic AI;

1.5 describe various possible tests for machine intelligence, outlining their strengths and weaknesses;

1.6 explain what is meant by the description of a digital computer as an 'interpreted automated formal system';

1.7 write a paragraph explaining the concepts of a computer model and of an optimisation problem;

1.8 distinguish between a simulation, a replication and an emulation;

1.9 write a few sentences distinguishing between strong and weak artificial intelligence, and explaining the goals of each.

2 Machines

2.1 The tool-building animal

It seems that one of humanity's most persistent dreams has been of artificial creatures, lifelike creations with the characteristics and powers of animals or humans: intelligent machines that are our servants, partners and even occasionally our enemies. Writing perhaps eight hundred years before the birth of Christ, the Greek bard Homer tells of how:

> Huge god Hephaestus got up from the anvil block
> with laboured breathing.
> At once he was helped along
> by female servants made of gold, who moved to him.
> They look like living servant girls, possessing minds,
> hearts with intelligence, vocal chords, and strength.
> They learned to work from the immortal gods.

Source: Homer, *Iliad* XVIII, translated by Ian Johnston (2002)

Hephaestus himself had built these beautiful robotic servants. He also created Talos (Figure 1.1), a gigantic mechanical man of bronze, the guardian of Crete, who ran round the entire coast of the island three times a day (this equates to a speed of 250 miles per hour!) and hurled great rocks at suspected intruders.

(a)   (b)

Figure 1.1   (a) The death of Talos as depicted on a Greek vase, c. 400 BC. (b) Talos as envisaged by Ray Harryhausen in the 1963 film *Jason and the Argonauts*

Nearly three thousand years later, Isaac Asimov imagined a world entirely run by benevolent, all-knowing machines in this dialogue between characters in his short story 'The Evitable Conflict':

> '... Stephen, if I am right, it means that the machine is conducting our future for us ... How do we know what the ultimate good of humanity will entail? We haven't at *our* disposal the infinite factors that the Machine has at *its*! ... We don't know. Only the machines know and they are going there and taking us with them.'
>
> 'But are you telling me, Susan, that ... humanity has lost its own say in its future?'
>
> 'It never had any really. It was always at the mercy of economic and sociological forces it did not understand ... Now the Machines understand them; and no one can stop them, since the Machines will deal with them ... having, as they do, the greatest of weapons at their disposal, the absolute control of our economy.'
>
> 'How horrible!'
>
> 'Perhaps how wonderful! Think, that for all time all conflicts are finally evitable. Only the Machines, from now on, are inevitable!'
>
> Source: Asimov (1950)

Whether you find such visions sinister or benign, history, literature and myth are littered with tales of artificial men and animals: slaves, enemies or merely curiosities. It's worth taking a brief look at a few of these in order to make some serious points about this dream.

Exercise 1.1

Spend about twenty minutes searching the Web to find some other examples of artificial creatures down the ages – in reality, legend, myth or fiction. Think carefully about alternative search terms before starting your search.

Discussion ....

It didn't take me long to come up with the following:

▶ *The Golem*. Jewish myths of the Golem became popular around the 10th century. In the best-known version, Rabbi Yehudah Levi ben Betzalel of Prague created an artificial man from river clay spread over a frame of tree branches and rags, to act as servant and protector of the city's Jewish poor. The Golem was brought alive by holy words chanted by the Rabbi. It could not speak, but understood and obeyed verbal commands written by the Rabbi on a piece of paper and placed in its mouth. The Golem developed a human personality, becoming proud and oppressive towards the very people it was supposed to protect. Eventually it had to be destroyed by its creator.

▶ *Talking heads*. In the 13th century, both the philosopher Albertus Magnus and the English scientist and monk Roger Bacon were rumoured to have created heads that could talk, dismissed as sacrilegious abominations by their contemporaries. By the late 16th and early 17th centuries, fake talking heads were appearing all over Europe. The novelist Miguel de Cervantes's hero Don Quixote and his squire Sancho Panza encounter one:

> The last questioner was Sancho, and his questions were, 'Head, shall I by any chance have another government? Shall I ever escape from the hard life of a squire? Shall I get back to see my wife and children?' To which the answer came, 'Thou shalt govern in thy house; and if thou returnest to it thou shalt see thy wife and children; and on ceasing to serve thou shalt cease to be a squire.'
>
> 'Good, by God!' said Sancho Panza; 'I could have told myself that ...'
>
> Source: Cervantes, *Don Quixote*, Chapter LVIII (1615)

The effect is brought about by means of a tube down to the floor below. Talking machines are now commonplace, as anyone who has stepped into a lift recently can confirm.

▶ *Automata.* Around 1495 Leonardo da Vinci constructed an automaton in the form of an armoured man, capable of moving its arms and head, sitting up, and simulating speech by opening and closing its mouth. However, the 18th century was the true golden age of automata, intricately built mechanical creatures, sometimes with amazing capabilities. The prince among automata builders was Jacques de Vaucanson (1709–1782), whose machines were displayed all over Europe, to kings and scientists, nobles and commoners. Voltaire described him as 'bold Vaucanson, rival to Prometheus', a man with the power to create life. Vaucanson built machines that played musical instruments with all the eloquence of a human player. His Automaton Flute Player, for example, was a life-sized wooden figure that could play twelve different melodies. Powered by three groups of three bellows, it had lips that opened and closed and moved backwards and forwards, and a movable tongue. Its seven levers, each encased in animal skin, simulated human fingers, giving the machine a human's soft touch.

Most famous of all, however, was Vaucanson's Duck (Figure 1.2), a gold-plated copper automaton, which quacked and swam, rose on its legs and, astoundingly, ate food out of the exhibitor's hand, digested it and excreted it. Vaucanson devised an elaborate system of internal pipes to achieve this, complete with a chemical digestive plant in the place of the stomach. The duck made its last appearance in the Paris exhibition of 1844, long after Vaucanson's death in 1782.

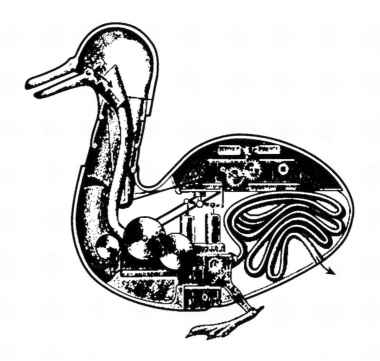

Figure 1.2   Inside Vaucanson's Duck

▶ *Game-playing automata.* Another favourite of the 18th and 19th century public were the machines apparently capable of playing board games, usually chess, against human opponents. The most famous of these, The Chess Automaton, better known as The Turk (Figure 1.3), was built by Baron Wolfgang Von Kempelen and toured Europe in the 1770s. The Turk was a wheeled wooden cabinet, with a chessboard and a life-sized wooden figure dressed in Turkish style mounted on its top. This machine offered to play chess against all comers, generally defeating them (its victims included Napoleon Bonaparte and Benjamin Franklin). As The Turk appeared to ponder, and then make, its move there would be an impressive mechanical clanking and a display of moving cogs. These, needless to say, had nothing to do with the machine's play: the cabinet concealed a human chess master. Such men had to be of small stature. Working by candlelight in conditions of appalling heat and cramp, playing the game and operating the mechanics of the robot arm, while covering up coughs and sneezes, not surprisingly many of them died early deaths from alcoholism or other illnesses. The chess genius and US Chess Champion, Harry Nelson Pillsbury, worked inside a later automaton, Ajeeb, for nearly ten years. He succumbed to syphilis in 1906 at the age of 34. Both The Turk and Ajeeb were eventually destroyed by fire.

Die Schachmaschine von Kempelen.

Figure 1.3   The Turk

All these contraptions were, of course, frauds. However, the 20th century has seen machines genuinely capable of beating human opponents at chess. In 1997, IBM's specialised computer Deep Blue beat the world chess champion Gary Kasparov in a six-game match. Since that epic struggle, Deep Blue's successors (Deep Junior, Deep Fritz and Hydra) have maintained a consistently good record against the highest-quality human opposition.

▶ *Robots.* Popular belief has it that the word 'robot' was coined by the Czech writer Karel Capek. In fact, the term was apparently invented by Capek's brother Josef; but the word did appear before the public for the first time in Karel Capek's 1920 play *RUR: Rossum's Universal Robots.* The literature of robots is immense, particularly in the 20th century, and there is no space to look at it here. The idea of machines in human form, stronger and maybe more intelligent than us, working with us as partners or slaves, seems to be endlessly fascinating.

Doubtless, you came up with several others.

Many of these contraptions might seem laughable – myths, dreams and deceptions of no relevance to a Computing course. But I think there are some serious points to be made here. These centre on three key questions:

1   Why build such artificial entities?

2   What sort of thing did people think these entities actually were?

3   What has been the public attitude to the idea of artificial creatures?

Let's consider each of these questions in turn.

Why build artificial creatures?

Or, in the case of the mythical creations I considered above, why imagine them being built? It's obvious that most of the examples I found were seen by their makers, and probably by the public too, simply as curiosities. One reason for building such lifelike machines, then, would have been to amuse, amaze, and milk money from the credulous – as in the case of the chess automata, or the talking heads. Another intention must surely have been to show off the skill and craftsmanship of the maker and thus to win aristocratic favour – Vaucanson's work is the obvious example of this. But I think we can also see two other clear purposes.

1 Firstly, humanity has always seen the potential for lifelike automata as *tools*. Imaginary creatures such as the Golem and Talos were protectors. Robots have always been imagined as humanity's servants, carrying out tasks humans are unwilling to do, and often with greater strength and dexterity than we ourselves could muster. Humans have been called 'tool-building animals'. Like every attempt to find a quality that uniquely defines humanity, this definition breaks down on closer inspection. Nevertheless, it is true that humans are by far the greatest tool builders in nature. The vision of the human-like machine is often simply a vision of another, powerful tool.

2 Secondly, the more serious builders of automata – again, Vaucanson is a prime example – saw themselves as conducting significant investigations into the nature of life itself. Vaucanson himself claimed that he was using methods that were 'copied from Nature', and there was much debate at the time about whether the new technologies helped to illuminate the gap between machines and living things. I'll return to this last point later.

What was being built? Or imagined?

The chess-playing automata were simple frauds – as their makers well knew. The idea was to *mimic* intelligent life, though the audience may have been willing to believe they were in the presence of a machine that was genuinely reasoning. On the other hand, mythical creations such as the Golem were imagined as being indisputably living things, capable of independent action and of real personality. Between these two extremes there is much less certainty. Clearly, Vaucanson's Duck was only an imitation of a real duck; but with its intricate internal mechanisms, did it in some way *approach* the reality? Would ever more complex mechanisms at some point result in a creature very like a real duck? Vaucanson himself believed he was imitating life. Descartes (of whom more later) believed that animal behaviour could be explained in purely mechanical terms. Could building a truly living creature some day be a possibility?

The crucial distinction here is between an original (a real duck) and an imitation or **simulacrum** of a duck. We can define a simulacrum as '… something having merely the form or appearance of a certain thing, without possessing its substance or proper qualities' (*Oxford English Dictionary*). So Vaucanson's Duck, according to this definition, is obviously a simulacrum. But could a *perfect* simulacrum ever be the *reality*? If it walks (exactly) like a duck and quacks (exactly) like a duck, could we ever claim it's a (real) duck? This distinction is not mere pedantry: it has been at the centre of many debates about artificial intelligence and will come up again in this course.

What has been the public attitude to artificial creatures?

Chess automata and mechanical animals astounded and delighted the 18th and 19th century public. However, the prospect of truly *humanoid* creations, with human powers, has always aroused much more mixed feelings.

SAQ 1.1

Look back at the brief quotation from Isaac Asimov's 'The Evitable Conflict'. What is your reaction to the vision of a world absolutely run by benevolent machines?

ANSWER...

Probably the same as mine: suspicion and hostility. Whatever humanity's shortcomings, and however great its ignorance, we would all prefer our fate to be in the hands of humans rather than machines.

A constant wavering between antagonism and approval runs through the history of humanity's long love affair with technology. The prospect of artificial creatures brings this ambivalence dramatically into the foreground. You'll recall that the Golem started as trusted protector of the Jews of Prague. However, it soon became a danger and had to be destroyed. To the extent that talking heads were believed in at all, they were seen as the work of the devil. The robots of Asimov's stories, although supposedly governed by iron laws preventing them from harming humans, all too often seem to be on the verge of running amok. Even today, many people are suspicious of the power of computers and of the role they play in our lives. And now, when at last we have a limited power to manipulate living things through gene technology, and perhaps to use this technology to tailor life to our needs, such work is widely believed to be a dangerous and immoral interference with nature.

2.2 Tools and machines

In the previous section I referred to one conception of humans as 'tool-building animals' and suggested that one of the motivations for an interest in constructing artificial creatures might simply be the desire to create more powerful and flexible tools. Consider this question.

SAQ 1.2

What, in the most general terms, is a tool?

ANSWER...

I would define a tool as any device that helps with the accomplishment of a task. Most physical tools (hammers, levers, screw presses, and so on) are objects that allow humans to increase the physical force they can exert, or to apply it in a more convenient way. Such tools are often referred to as **machines**.

The whole history of technology is one of machine building. Humans have limited strength compared to many animals, and traditionally we have used animals for tasks that require great power and effort. But we have also learned to build machines that enable us to multiply that strength and deploy it to maximum advantage. So it seems quite reasonable to imagine machines in the form of humans and animals, perhaps stronger, more nimble and less vulnerable than their natural counterparts, capable of extending the power and reach of humans.

Every age in human history has had its own dominant technologies, and the machines of each age will embody these. It is only natural, then, that the lifelike machines imagined by every era have been pictured in terms of the technology of the time. Homer, writing about (although not living in) the Bronze Age, was bound to picture Hephaestus's handmaidens as creatures of gold; and the early Greeks could only have imagined Talos as a bronze warrior.

The 17th and 18th centuries – the period of the **Enlightenment**, Europe's great **Age of Reason** – saw the dominance of clockwork mechanisms. Vaucanson himself soon abandoned automata building (although it had made him a rich man) and applied the principles he had learned to the development of mechanised tools, inventing the world's first completely automated loom, controlled by a punch-card technology that anticipated the computer by two centuries. He also invented a revolutionary kind of lathe.

So dominant was the 18th century mechanical picture that thinkers of the time frequently described the universe itself in terms of the metaphor of a great clock, an intricate mechanism moving with the perfect regularity and predictability of clockwork. The French mathematician Pierre Simon Laplace (1749–1827) wrote:

> An intellect which at a certain moment would know all forces that set nature in motion, and all positions of all items of which nature is composed, if this intellect were also vast enough to submit these data to analysis, it would embrace in a single formula the movements of the greatest bodies of the universe and those of the tiniest atom; for such an intellect nothing would be uncertain and the future just like the past would be present before its eyes.

> Source: Laplace, *Celestial Mechanics* (1799–1825)

So what could have been more natural than to picture the workings of human and animal bodies also as clockwork mechanisms? And to build copies of these that were believed to mimic nature?

Perhaps one of the most influential thinkers to envisage human and animal bodies as analogous to clockwork machines was René Descartes (1596–1650). Descartes wrote:

> I suppose the body to be nothing but a statue or machine made of earth ... Thus God ... places inside it all the parts required to make it walk, eat, breathe and indeed to imitate all those of our functions that can be imagined to proceed from matter ... .

> We see clocks, artificial fountains, mills and other such machines which, although only man made, have power to move of their own accord in many different ways. But I am supposing this machine to be made by the hands of God, and so ... you may reasonably think it capable of a greater variety of movements than I could possibly imagine in it ... .

> Source: Descartes, *Treatise on Man* (1664)

Figure 1.4
René Descartes

Writing later, Julien Offray de La Mettrie (1709–1751), a physician with detailed knowledge of human anatomy, stated baldly that '... the human body is a self-winding machine, a living representation of perpetual motion'.

SAQ 1.3

If human and animal bodies are essentially just machines, do you think anything follows from this?

ANSWER...

If human and animal bodies are indeed merely very complex machines then it seems a logical next step to say that, with sufficiently powerful technology, perfect copies of such bodies could, in principle, be built.

But this immediately raises an overpowering thought. What is it that most clearly characterises humans as 'tool-building animals'? The obvious answer is the ingenuity that enables humans to conceive, design and build tools in the first place – human *intelligence*. If artificial human bodies could, in principle, be constructed, what about minds? Would it be possible to build an *artificial intelligence*?

3 | Minds

The limitations of the 18th century automata are obvious. Perhaps they are best summed up in the 20th-century mathematician Norbert Wiener's words:

> Let us consider the activity of the little figures which dance on top of a music box. They move in accordance with a pattern which is set in advance, and in which the past activity of the figure has practically nothing to do with the pattern of the future activity. The probability that they will diverge from the pattern is nil.
>
> Source: Norbert Wiener, *The Human Use of Human Beings* (1950)

This was as obvious to the people of the 18th century as it is to us. It was clear to them that mechanical automata, and probably animals too, lacked something crucial – some animating spark, some vital force, that would enable them to act intelligently and purposefully on their own. They lacked the quality of **agency**. They lacked minds.

3.1 | What is mind?

So the question was, and is, where does mind come from? What is it? To early civilisations, without complex technologies, mind and agency were ultimately mysterious, to be explained only in terms of spirits and the work of gods. In the legend of Talos, the mighty bronze warrior had a single vein passing from his neck to his ankle, closed off by one bronze nail in the ankle, through which flowed a divine, animating substance called *ichor*. The Golem was merely clay: it only achieved agency through the spirit breathed into it by the rabbi.

Even Descartes could not bring himself to accept that mind could have a mechanical origin. Although he saw both animal and human bodies as machines, he distinguished between animal behaviour, which is simply mechanical, and *intelligent* behaviour which he believed only humans are capable of:

> It is also a very remarkable fact that although many animals show more skill than we do in some of their actions, yet the same animals show none at all in many others; so what they do better does not prove they have any intelligence ... It proves rather that they have no intelligence at all, and it is nature which acts in them according to the disposition of their organs. In the same way a clock, consisting only of wheels and springs, can count the hours and measure time more accurately than we can with all our wisdom.

> After that, I described the rational soul ... that ... cannot be derived in any way from the potentiality of matter. And I showed ... it must be ...closely joined and united with the body in order to have ... feelings and appetites ... and so constitute a real man.
>
> Source: Descartes, *Discourse on the Method*, VI (1637)

Descartes was what philosophers call a **dualist**. He believed that the mind and the body are completely different kinds of thing. For him, humans – and only humans – could be intelligent. Only humans had a rational soul, a non-material, immortal, thinking spirit inhabiting their bodies.

But others were prepared to go where Descartes could not, to think the unthinkable and entertain the idea that mind might also have a purely physical, mechanical origin. La Mettrie, who I mentioned earlier, ended his work *Machine Man* with a bold claim:

> Let us, therefore, conclude boldly that man is a machine, and that the universe contains only one single, diversely modified substance.

Source: La Mettrie, *Machine Man* (1747)

This is in clear contrast to Descartes' dualism. La Mettrie was a **monist** and a **materialist**, holding that there is only *one* kind of substance in the universe – matter – and that thus, ultimately, both mind and body must spring from the same material causes. This philosophical debate between monism and dualism has persisted, in various forms, to the present day, without real resolution. We will have to leave it there.

However, given the theme of our course, the key figure is the 17th-century thinker Thomas Hobbes (1588–1679). Like La Mettrie, Hobbes also believed that the mind was a material, mechanical thing, made of the same stuff as the body:

Figure 1.5
Thomas Hobbes

> All ... qualities called sensible are in the object that causeth them [nothing] but so many several motions of the matter, by which it presseth our organs diversely. Neither in us that are pressed are they anything else but diverse motions (for motion produceth nothing but motion).

Source: Hobbes, *Leviathan*, I (1651)

In other words, motions in the objects around us excite our senses and cause resonances in the particles that make up our minds. So, mind is just another material thing, like the body. But Hobbes went further: he claimed that the operations of the mind – what he called *ratiocination*, and which we can take to mean reasoning or thinking – was a form of *computation*. He wrote:

> By ratiocination, I mean *computation*. Now to compute is either to collect the sum of many things that are added together, or to know what remains when one thing is taken out of another. Ratiocination, therefore, is the same with addition and subtraction.

Source: Hobbes, *Elements of Philosophy Concerning Body* (1656)

So, thinking, for Hobbes, was just another form of arithmetic, but performed with concepts and ideas rather than with numbers. He goes on:

> We must not think that computation, that is ratiocination, has a place only in numbers, as if man were distinguished from other living creatures ... by nothing but the faculty of numbering; for *magnitude*, *body*, *motion*, *time* ... *action*, *conception*, ... *speech* and *names* ... are capable of addition and subtraction. Now such things as we add or subtract, ... we are said to *consider* ... to *compute*, *reason* or *reckon*.

Source: Hobbes, *Elements of Philosophy Concerning Body* (1656)

Even more significantly, Hobbes wrote:

> When man reasoneth, he does nothing else but conceive a sum total, from addition of parcels; or conceive a remainder, from subtraction of one sum from another: which, if it be done by words, is conceiving of the consequence of the names of all the parts, to the name of the whole ... .

Source: Hobbes, *Leviathan*, V (1651)

Hobbes' sentences are difficult to unpick, but we need only focus on one word here: 'parcel'. If we substitute a modern word for this – *symbol* – we can try to summarise Hobbes' position simply and in more contemporary language.

Exercise 1.2

Try to sum up what Hobbes was trying to say about the nature of mind and thinking. He is a difficult writer, especially to modern readers, so you need only be quite general.

Discussion ....

I thought perhaps the best way to sum it up is in a list:

▶ The world consists only of particles of matter in motion.

▶ Bodies and minds are also just particles of matter in motion. Their motions are caused, in part, by the effects of the movements of particles outside the body, which press on the senses, causing particles in our minds to move in sympathy.

▶ The particles in our minds form parcels: that is, symbols representing concepts such as number, time, names, and so on.

▶ Thought amounts to a form of computation, in which these mental symbols are added, subtracted, etc., in processes similar to those of arithmetic.

In short, for Hobbes, intelligent activity consists in a *material body* of some kind, using clear rules to manipulate internal *physical symbols* that stand for *objects* in the world. In principle, then, artificial minds could be built. And another serious question is raised by Hobbes' theory, too, although the philosopher might not have been aware of it. If thinking is essentially the manipulation of physical tokens that represent features of the world, then does it matter what those tokens actually *are*? They may be features of the brain in humans; but might they not equally be beads, tin cans or electric currents?

However, there is little evidence that any of the Enlightenment scientists seriously entertained the idea that an artificial mind might be built. As I suggested earlier, our view of ourselves as humans, and of artificial creatures that might resemble us, has always been conditioned by the technologies of our age. The science of the 17th and 18th centuries was not really up to the task of providing an adequate picture of how a thinking artefact might be constructed. This was to be left to a later era, with new technologies, which yielded new ways of thinking about the mind. But it was the philosophers of the Age of Reason who laid the intellectual foundations of one of the 20th century's great projects – **artificial intelligence**.

3.2 Artificial intelligence

New eras bring new technologies. But our own age, the 20th and 21st centuries, has been an age of technology developing at bewildering speed.

Exercise 1.3

Note down what you think are a few of the dominant technologies of the last hundred years.

Discussion ....

Actually, this is quite a tricky question. In an era like our own, it's difficult to single out any one technology that has dominated, since there are so many and the speed of change is so great. You may have considered energy technologies, such as electricity or nuclear power; or mechanical ones, including the internal combustion engine and the jet; or medical ones, such as vaccination or antibiotics. Maybe you thought of mass-communication technologies, including radio and television. However, it's not possible to look at the applied science of the latter half of the 20th and the early 21st centuries without considering electronics, electronic communication and the digital computer.

In the years between the end of the 18th century and the middle of the 20th, the dream of an artificial mind had not been forgotten. The mathematician George Boole (1815–1864) attempted to give precision to Hobbes' insights into thinking as a form of computation, by developing a mathematical account of logical thinking known as **Boolean algebra**, in his book *Laws of Thought* (1854). This work profoundly influenced some of the pioneers of artificial intelligence. Meanwhile, advances in engineering technology made it possible for Boole's contemporary, Charles Babbage (1791–1871), to design, and try to build, the first recognisable *computers*:

1　*The Difference Engine*, intended to be used for calculating mathematical tables, was abandoned incomplete in 1823, after the huge sum of £23,000 had been spent on it.

2　*The Analytical Engine* of 1835 was, arguably, the first programmable computer. If it had been constructed as Babbage designed it, the Engine would have been over eight metres long, with 24,000 parts. However, Babbage was not able to raise sufficient money to build the machine; he abandoned work on it in 1843 in favour of a different design.

3　*The Second Analytical Engine* was designed by Babbage in 1849. It was a much more compact and efficient design, with only about 8000 parts. But again, no money was forthcoming for actual construction. However, in 1991 the London Science Museum built a full-scale working replica based on Babbage's plans.

However, it was not until the advent of the electronic technologies of the 20th century that artificial intelligence at last seemed as if it might become a reality. Mid-century, and within ten years of one another, two movements emerged with this general aim in mind: **Cybernetics** and **AI**. These two movements are so important to the argument of this course that they both deserve detailed consideration.

3.3 | Cybernetics

It's difficult to sum up the goals and inspirations of Cybernetics in a single neat word or phrase. Historians of science acknowledge the mathematician and physicist Norbert Wiener (1894–1964) as the intellectual father of the field. It was he who coined the term 'cybernetics' for his new thinking – the word first appears in Plato in the sense of 'the art of navigation' and was also used by the Enlightenment scientist André-Marie Ampère to mean 'the science of government'. During the Second World War, Wiener had worked in gunnery control, on a device that would automatically track an enemy aircraft, predict its path across the sky and keep an anti-aircraft gun continuously aimed at it. Although the machine was never fully constructed, Wiener gained an important insight from it. It was clear to him that such a device was not a simple automaton, like Vaucanson's creations; unlike them, in a very rudimentary way it seemed to be acting purposefully, as if it had agency. How was this possible? Wiener wrote afterwards:

> I came to the conclusion that an extremely important factor in voluntary activity is what control engineers term *feedback* … . It is enough to say here that when we desire a motion to follow a given pattern, the difference between this pattern and the actually performed motion is used as a new input to cause the part regulated to move in such a way as to bring its motion closer to that given by the pattern … .
>
> Source: Wiener, *Cybernetics* (1948)

The concept of **feedback** is so central to Cybernetics and to new trends in artificial intelligence that we should dwell on it for a moment.

Figure 1.6
Norbert Wiener

Exercise 1.4

Try to come up with your own definition of feedback. Use a dictionary, or search the Web if you want, but use your own words as far as possible.

Discussion ....

Most definitions seem to agree on the central idea that feedback is a process in which all or part of the output of a system is passed back to become its input. However, this seems to me to miss something of what Wiener was trying to say. I'll return to this point shortly.

The use of feedback as a means of control had been known for some time. A classic example, quoted in most textbooks, is the *steam governor*. Eighteenth-century engineers working with steam engines were faced with the problem of controlling the flow of steam that determined the speed of an engine. If too much steam entered its cylinders it would turn too fast, and might possibly break down under the strain. If too little entered, then it would run too slowly. The aim was to keep the engine running at a constant speed, by continuously monitoring the rate at which it was turning, and opening or closing a valve to increase or diminish the inward flow of steam, as required.

Of course, high-speed electronic monitoring technology was unknown at the time, so at first this seemed an intractable problem. However, in 1787 the Scottish engineer James Watt patented a solution that was beautiful in its elegance and simplicity – the centrifugal steam governor (Figure 1.7).

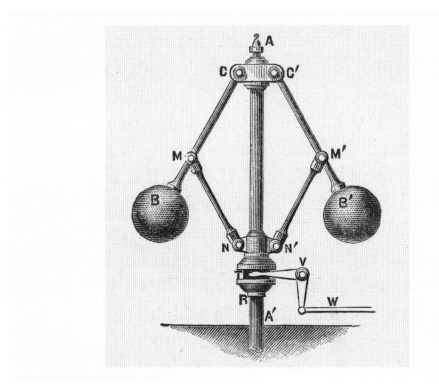

Figure 1.7   Example of a centrifugal steam governor

The device used two heavy balls, mounted on arms that were free to swing inwards or outwards. These arms were connected to a regulator that opened or closed the steam valve, and also to the main drive shaft, so the arm assembly rotated at the same speed as the engine. If the engine started to turn too fast, centrifugal force drove the balls and arms upwards and outwards in wider circles. This caused the steam valve to close, choking off the flow of steam and thus reducing speed. As the engine's speed diminished, the balls lowered, the valve re-opened and more steam was admitted, speeding the engine up again. In practice the device responded instantly to changes in engine speed and was able to preserve a constant rate. The centrifugal governor can still be seen on steam engines. It is a perfect example of **negative feedback**.

But I think there was slightly more in what Wiener was claiming for his anti-aircraft predictor. At the start of this section I quoted briefly from his comments on the fixed patterns of the automaton – you can take a quick look back at this if you want. Wiener continued this line of thought as follows:

> The figures themselves have no trace of communication with the outer world, except in this one-way stage of communication with the established mechanism of the music box. They are blind, deaf and dumb and cannot in any way vary their activity in the least from the conventional pattern.

> Source: Wiener, *The Human Use of Human Beings* (1950)

Now, in the case of the anti-aircraft predictor, where would the feedback come from? Not from anywhere in the device itself, but from the motion of the aircraft across the sky. The machine constantly adjusts its prediction and its aim as it gets fresh feedback information on the actual movements of the aircraft. The main point about this kind of feedback, then, is that it comes from the *environment outside* the machine. The device is in constant contact with the world around it. This idea will take on major importance in Block 3.

After the war, a group of major talents assembled around the banner of Cybernetics. These included neurophysiologists Warren McCullough and Grey Walter, mathematicians Walter Pitts and John von Neumann, the engineer Julian Bigelow, the psychiatrist William Ross Ashby, and others including anthropologists, physicists and economists. As I claimed above, it's difficult to find a neat paraphrase of the movement's aims. As you can see, Cybernetics was from the start a multidisciplinary project, an abstract study belonging to no particular field. Wiener himself described **Cybernetics** as:

> ... a new field in science. It combines under one heading the study of what in a human context is sometimes loosely described as thinking and in engineering is known as control and communication. In other words, cybernetics attempts to find the common elements in the functioning of automatic machines and of the human nervous system, and to develop a theory that will cover the entire field of control and communication in machines and in living organisms.

> Source: Wiener, *Cybernetics* (1948)

An ambitious programme indeed. The goal of Cybernetics was to find a complete theoretical account of the mechanisms such as feedback that enable animals (and possibly machines) to act independently and purposefully. It was a study of the machinery of agency and intelligence.

There is no space for a history of Cybernetics here. The group had some successes, in particular McCullough and Pitts' work on the computing capacities of artificial nervous systems, which you will meet again in Block 4. However, it is fair to say that by the late 1950s its star was sinking. It was being challenged by a new and exciting perspective on mechanised thought – **AI**.

4 AI

4.1 Enter the digital computer

You might be a touch puzzled at this point. So far, I've been talking about artificial intelligence as one of the major intellectual projects of the 20th century, with roots stretching back to the 17th century and earlier. Now I'm introducing *AI* as if it was something quite different. Doesn't AI just stand for artificial intelligence?

It does; but in M366 the authors are going to use the term AI, or more specifically **Symbolic AI**, to refer to something slightly narrower – to a particular *branch* of artificial intelligence that began in the early 1940s and continues to this day, an *approach* to the goal of building intelligent machines that has certain specific assumptions and strategies. From now on, and throughout M366, we will use the term 'Symbolic AI' to refer to a thread running through the broader project of artificial intelligence: it is not the whole project itself. The purpose of this section is to reveal what the principles and goals of Symbolic AI are.

Figure 1.8
Alan Turing

Symbolic AI is generally reckoned to have been born in1956, at the 'Dartmouth Summer Research Project on Artificial Intelligence' in New Hampshire, USA. However, this is a US-centric view of history. In fact, Symbolic AI was being discussed in Britain as early as 1941. During the Second World War, the great English mathematician Alan Turing – often described as 'the father of AI' (and of 'artificial life' and of computing itself) – was working at Bletchley Park, Britain's wartime code-breaking centre, where some of the earliest computers were built. There, his colleagues recall, he circulated a paper (now lost) on the subject of machine intelligence. The question of the possible construction of machines capable of playing chess was also freely discussed among the code-breakers. In 1948, Turing set out his ideas in an extraordinarily far-sighted paper 'Intelligent Machinery', which not only anticipated Symbolic AI, but also built on cyberneticists McCullough and Pitts' work on artificial nervous systems. In 1951, the first chess-playing program, written by Dietrich Prinz, was running on a computer at Manchester University. A draughts program was devised by Christopher Sylvester in the same year and ran successfully on the Manchester computer in 1952. Systems incorporating simple forms of learning appeared on Cambridge University computers in 1951. Britain had an early lead in computer technology and in artificial intelligence which it soon lost.

In the United States scientists were also quick to realise the potential of the new computing technologies. At the 1956 summer conference at Dartmouth Naval College, the whole question of thinking machines was discussed. It was here that the term 'artificial intelligence', coined by John McCarthy, made its first appearance.

Exercise 1.5

Read quickly through the document **Dartmouth.pdf** on the course DVD. This is an edited extract from the original proposal for the Dartmouth conference.

Try to sum up what you think the authors propose as the main goals of the general problem of building intelligent programs. What approaches to these goals do they consider? Some of the later pages are rather technical, but don't get bogged down in these – just try to extract what you think are the main points.

Discussion ....

Despite the fact that this is an edited version of the original, it is still quite a complex document. Here are what I thought were some of the most important points, ones which I'll expand on in the rest of the unit and which will come up again throughout the course.

First of all, the authors focus on certain features of human intelligence:

▶ use of language

▶ forming and using concepts

▶ complex problem-solving, such as playing chess

▶ learning

▶ creativity.

Constructing machines that have these features is the goal of Symbolic AI.

The authors suggest some of the approaches to this problem that they believe might be most effective. I particularly noted the following:

1 *Search*. Machines can locate the answer to a problem by sifting systematically through all possible answers and selecting the correct (or the best) one. This idea had already been suggested by Turing, influenced very strongly by his wartime work on code-breaking machines.

2 *Symbols and rules*. In discussing the possibility of machines' use of language, the authors conjecture that computers can be programmed to manipulate words (symbols) according to logical and linguistic rules.

3 *Mathematical structure*. Later in the paper McCarthy writes of aspects of his own work. Among the points he raises is the question of how brains form models of the environment around them. His assumption seems to be that any model formed by a *computer* of its environment must be a logical or mathematical structure of some kind: 'The emphasis here is on clarifying the environmental model, and representing it as a mathematical structure'.

4 *Randomness*. The authors suggest that the problem of creativity in machines could be handled by injecting some degree of randomness into the orderly processes of the computer.

5 *'Neuron networks'*. Insights into the workings of human intelligence can be found, the authors suggest, by simulating on computers the structures found in the brain. This is a major theme of the course; but, oddly enough, as you'll see, this idea lay dormant for many years.

Finally, I was struck by one crucial proposal – that Symbolic AI should start with very simple problems and environments and work up to ones that are the most complex and challenging:

> Often in discussing mechanized intelligence, we think of machines performing the most advanced human thought activities – proving theorems, writing music, or playing chess. I am proposing here to start at the simple ... to work up through a series of easy stages in the direction of these advanced activities.
>
> Source: McCarthy et al. (1955)

Some of these proposals were not followed up; others came to be the core of Symbolic AI research in the ensuing decades. To simplify the above discussion, just let me isolate two key principles which certainly did become central – these are:

1 **Representation**. 'Intelligent' computer systems contain a *model*, in some logical or mathematical form, of the problem being solved, or of their environment. These models are thus essentially *symbolic*, consisting, as they do, of logical expressions.

2   **Search**. Computer systems can find 'intelligent' answers to complex problems by searching among all possible answers for the best one. The process of search will be governed by *rules*.

These may sound rather abstract at this point. Later in this unit I'll return to the question of what, exactly, symbols, rules and models are. Block 2 contains abundant discussion and examples of the principles of representation and search.

SAQ 1.4

Very briefly summarise the distinction that is being made by the M366 authors between artificial intelligence and Symbolic AI.

ANSWER..

For us, Symbolic AI is a study of the technological questions surrounding the possible replication of human intelligence on digital computers, using principles of representation and search. Artificial intelligence is a much wider quest, of which Symbolic AI is a part, to build intelligent machines.

Up to now we seem to have been assuming that it's clear what an intelligent machine is, and how we would recognise one if we saw it. But are the answers to these questions really so obvious?

What is intelligence?

This is a course about artificial intelligence. The aim of artificial intelligence is simply this: *to build intelligent machines*. This goal seems ambitious enough and is certainly easy to state. But before we can even start on such a project, we must have a fairly clear idea of what it really is we are trying to build. We all think we know what a machine is and we all probably feel we can recognise intelligence when we meet it. But maybe this confidence is misplaced? There are two major questions we have to try and settle before we embark. They are:

1   What is intelligence anyway?

2   If we did manage to build an intelligent machine, how could we tell if it was really intelligent?

Alone, these two seemingly simple questions have spawned a vast literature. However, I only want to deal with them quite briefly, for reasons that I hope will become clear soon, and as a means of making three important observations. Let's start with an exercise that one can find in every course in artificial intelligence.

Exercise 1.6

What do you think intelligence is? Jot down a few notes about this.

Discussion ....

The number of possible answers you might have come up with is bewildering. It's possible you offered alternative *names* for the concept, such as 'ingenuity', 'nous', 'cleverness', and so on. But it's likely that you also backed that up with a fuller *description* or *definition*, perhaps something along the lines of 'the capacity to think and reason', 'the ability to apply knowledge' or some such. Most likely of all, though, is that you suggested *examples* of intelligence, such as logical reasoning, use of language, abstract thought, and so on.

Although we may all think we recognise intelligence when we see it, it seems to be a difficult notion to pin down. In the discussion above, I suggested three overlapping approaches one might take to defining the concept: names, definitions and descriptions. But there are objections to the kinds of answers all these three lead to:

1   *Names*. Suggesting names or synonyms for intelligence gets us no further, really. Saying that 'intelligence' is the same as 'cleverness' hardly tells us anything of interest.

2   *Definitions*. Obviously this is a better idea, but still runs into trouble. For a start, there's little obvious agreement on a definition. A Google search I carried out yielded – after discounting special meanings, such as 'spying' – ten or more competing definitions, among them:

    ▶   the ability to comprehend; to understand and profit from experience (http://wordnet.princeton.edu/perl/webwn);

    ▶   a general mental capability that involves the ability to reason, plan, solve problems, think abstractly, comprehend ideas and language, and learn (http://en.wikipedia.org/wiki/Intelligence_(trait));

    ▶   the ability of an individual to understand and cope with the environment (http://www.upei.ca/~xliu/measurement/glossary.htm);

    ▶   the capacity to create constructively for the purpose of evolutionary gain (http://www.eoni.com/~visionquest/library/glossary.html).

    Several things strike me about these. Leaving aside the obvious disagreements (in some cases they hardly seem to be talking about the same thing at all), a second point is that they all seem very *abstract*: intelligence is defined in terms of other concepts – 'comprehension', 'understanding', 'reasoning', 'creativity' – which are equally vague. A third related point – slightly less obvious, perhaps – is *circularity*. Defining 'intelligence' in such terms as 'comprehension', or 'thinking abstractly', words which we inevitably associate with intelligence anyway, is to some extent saying little more than 'intelligence is behaving intelligently'.

3   *Examples*. Most definitions of abstract concepts rely on examples. To define 'intelligence', it is only natural to fall back on instances of what we take to be intelligent *behaviour*: reasoning, problem solving, use of language, and so on. This is clearly helpful, but has its own problems. Maybe to single out two or three examples of intelligent behaviour as defining properties of 'intelligence' is to be in danger of ignoring others. Suppose we take 'abstract reasoning' as a core property of intelligence: what about the quick-thinking solver of practical problems? Alternatively, suppose we take 'use of language' as key: does this mean the tongue-tied mathematical genius is more stupid than the silver-tongued political rabble-rouser? This may seem like hair-splitting. However, I'll argue later that to define intelligence in terms of just a few key abilities may be to make a serious mistake.

So what about *artificial* intelligence, the quest to build intelligent machines? You'll find most books on the subject start with a brief attempt to define what it is that practitioners are trying to do. To produce a long list of these would be wearying, so here are just three examples:

> [The automation of] activities we associate with human thinking, activities such as decision-making, problem solving, learning ...
>
> Source: Bellman, *An Introduction to Artificial Intelligence* (1978)

> The study of computations that make it possible to perceive, reason and act.
>
> Source: Winston, *Artificial Intelligence* (1992)

> The design and study of computer programs that behave intelligently. These programs are constructed to perform as would a human or animal whose behaviour we consider intelligent.
>
> Source: Dean et al., *Artificial Intelligence: Theory and practice* (1995)

All the problems I outlined above are here: disagreement, abstractness, circularity, a reliance on a few key examples. But my aim is not to belittle these authors – I certainly could have done no better myself. I just want to make three observations about the whole endeavour, which I think relate to the foundations of the whole project of artificial intelligence.

Observation 1: There is an obvious lack of agreement on what intelligence is, and thus of the exact goals of artificial intelligence.

Observation 2: The only really clear and effective definitions of intelligence are in terms of a few *examples* of intelligent behaviour: perception, reasoning and action, in the case of Winston above; decision making, problem solving and learning in Bellman's definition.

Observation 3: The overwhelming focus is on *human* intelligence. You may recall that Descartes considered animals to be simply mindless automata. The quotation from Hobbes' *Elements of Philosophy* above suggests that Hobbes too thought our intelligence made us utterly distinct from the animal world. Bellman and Winston above seem to concentrate on human qualities such as reasoning and problem-solving and most other authors follow them. Only Dean et al. gave explicit consideration to the view that non-human animals are capable of intelligence too. The intelligence of animals, which I am calling **natural intelligence**, is a major theme of this course.

Actually, one of the most honest comments I've read on the actual practice of artificial intelligence comes from Russell and Norvig:

> We have now explained why AI is exciting, but we have not said what it *is*. We could just say, 'Well it has to do with smart programs, so let's get on and write some.'
>
> Source: Russell and Norvig, *Artificial Intelligence: A modern approach* (1995)

As a computer scientist myself, I sympathise with this. But suppose I do write a system of some kind that I'm claiming is intelligent. How could I tell if it was intelligent?

Exercise 1.7

Suggest a few ways it might be possible to tell if a computer system is intelligent. You might find it helpful to consider why you consider your friends and colleagues are intelligent (if indeed you do).

Discussion ....

Of course, as before we're hampered by uncertainty about the meaning of the term 'intelligence'. It's instructive, though, to ask why it is we believe other humans, our friends and acquaintances, possess that basic human quality. Well, I can't *know* for certain that my best friend is an intelligent, reasoning human being, rather than a brilliantly constructed but mindless automaton. But I can *assume* it from her *actions*. She holds conversations, responds appropriately and flexibly to the world about her, solves problems, plans ahead, turns up for appointments at the right time, pursues her own goals, etc.

An answer like this looks quite convincing, but may run into some of the same problems we ran into in trying to define intelligence in the first place. I suggested a whole list of *actions* by which I might judge my friend to be intelligent. But did I leave any out? Are some of the actions I did mention more important than others? Am I promoting some at the expense of others?

This is not a modern problem. Descartes faced up to it in the 17th century, as he pondered the differences between humans and animals. And his answer has had such an immense influence on the founders (and later practitioners) of Symbolic AI, that I think it is worth looking at closely. He wrote:

> ... if there were machines which had ... the external shape of a monkey or of some other animal without reason, we would have no way of recognizing that they were not exactly the same nature as the animals; whereas, if there was a machine shaped like our bodies which imitated our actions ... we would always have two very certain ways of recognizing that they were not ... true human beings.

> The first of these is that they would never be able to use words ... as we do to declare our thoughts to others: for one can easily imagine a machine made in such a way that it expresses words, ... but one cannot imagine a machine that arranges words in various ways to reply to the sense of everything said in its presence, as the most stupid human beings are capable of doing.

> The second test is that, although these machines might do several things as well or perhaps better than we do, they are inevitably lacking in some other, through which we discover that they act, not by knowledge, but only by the arrangement of their organs ... As a result of that, it is morally impossible that there is in a machine's organs sufficient variety to act in all the events of our lives in the same way that our reason empowers us to act.

> Now, by these two same means, one can also recognize the difference between human beings and animals. For it is really remarkable that there are no men so dull and stupid, including even idiots, who are not capable of putting together different words and of creating out of them a conversation through which they make their thoughts known ...

Source: Descartes, *Discourse on the Method*, V (1637)

Despite the elegant 17th-century language, this passage has an extraordinarily modern ring. Descartes saw very clearly some of the problems and challenges of modern artificial intelligence. So, it is worth being very clear about the points he is making.

SAQ 1.5

Sum up the two tests Descartes proposes for detecting true intelligence.

ANSWER..

The first test is the ability to use *language*. Humans alone, who are for Descartes the only creatures capable of intelligence, can put together words so flexibly as to be able to respond to the infinite variety of situations that confront them. A trained animal, or an automaton, he believes, is bound sooner or later to be caught out.

Secondly, humans are *versatile*. We are always capable of acting flexibly and creatively in novel situations.

In the last paragraph, he suggests, once again, that it is the use of language that can bo used as a test for the existence of reason.

As I've argued, Descartes' concentration on language performance had a huge influence on the founding fathers of artificial intelligence. One can see strong echoes of it in the Dartmouth proposal paper you dealt with in Exercise 1.5, with its stress on language, creativity and problem solving as key features of intelligence. But without doubt the dominant influence on modern thinking about recognising intelligence, human and artificial, and the direct heir of Descartes, was Alan Turing.

In his seminal 1950 paper 'Computing machinery and intelligence', Turing addressed the same question Descartes had faced three hundred years earlier. What are the defining features of intelligence and how can we recognise them? But for Turing, the matter had real urgency, because he believed that in the *digital computer* we had at last found a machine that could be made intelligent. We will return to the issue of what was Turing's exact idea of the digital computer later in this unit. For the moment, let's consider how he tackled the question of how intelligence could be recognised.

Exercise 1.8

Read through the first five sections of Turing's paper 'Computing machinery and intelligence' (the course DVD will give you instructions on how to acquire this). You might care to read the full text of the paper, if you have time. What test does Turing propose for the detection of intelligence in a machine?

Discussion ....

Turing proposed an investigation that he called the 'Imitation Game', but which is now famously called the **Turing Test**. In Turing's game, there are two channels of communication, A and B, through to a neutral human observer, C: A comes from a computer and B from an average human being, but C has no knowledge of which is which, as both are hidden and communicate through a standard teletype. The job of the computer at A is, in a dialogue with C, to convince her that it is a human being. C is free to ask any questions, or make any remarks, she likes in the dialogue, and to go on for as long as she wants; but if in the end she is unable to tell which is the human and which the computer, then the computer has passed the Turing Test and can be said to be intelligent.

You should be able to see clearly the influence of Descartes here. For Turing, as for Descartes, the key indicator of intelligence is flexibility of response through language. Turing's proposal has been immensely influential and, although many modern researchers believe it is deeply flawed, as a definitive test for intelligence in machines it has never been seriously challenged. In 1990 Hugh Loebner, in collaboration with the Cambridge Center for Behavioral Studies, set up a yearly competition for The Loebner Prize. He provided the capital for a gold medal and an award of US$ 100,000 to the programmers of the first computer to pass the Turing Test by giving responses indistinguishable from a human's. The prize has not yet been won (2006). However, each year a prize of $2000 and a bronze medal is presented to the designers of the most human computer program, as compared to other entries that year.

Figure 1.9   A light-hearted view of The Turing Test

Exercise 1.9

Read through the document **Loebner.pdf** on the course DVD. These are (lightly edited) transcripts of some of the dialogues between the human judge and the winning computer in 2005, a program called Jabberwacky. I've also included one transcript of a conversation with the human confederate B. Can you tell which of the transcripts is the one of the dialogue with the human confederate? How well does Jabberwacky perform in the Turing Test, in your opinion? What do you think is its chief failing?

Discussion ....

It was fairly obvious to me that the only dialogue involving a human was Transcript 2. It's possible that you didn't spot it, but this doesn't necessarily mean any shortcoming on your part. However, I think it does point to a weakness of the Turing Test itself: it is really quite *subjective* – what seems natural and human to you may seem artificial and machine-like to me. More importantly, one can argue that we (all of us) subconsciously *want* to be fooled: our tendency is always to read order, pattern and rationality into the situations we encounter, even if they are not present, in just the same way as we see faces and images in the random patterns of the clouds.

It's hard to make a clear judgement of Jabberwacky's performance. Sometimes the replies seem quite normal and human. At other times they seem wildly off the mark, almost random. A general tendency of all systems designed to pass the Turing Test is that they work reasonably well so long as the dialogue follows predictable, standard lines. However, if the observer is prepared to challenge the system, by responding unpredictably, not cooperating, and so on, then the machine soon starts to reveal itself as just that – a machine.

Whatever its shortcomings, the Turing Test remains a gold standard within artificial intelligence for the recognition of intelligence, if only because no one has been able to propose a satisfactory alternative. However, if you look back quickly at the earlier section on the background to Symbolic AI, you might detect one other test of intelligence that the early researchers had in mind.

SAQ 1.6

From your readings so far, can you think of other indications of intelligence that have often been suggested?

ANSWER...

You may have thought of several possible answers here. However, one does stand out for me: the pioneers of Symbolic AI were particularly interested in the idea that the ability to play *chess* is a clear indicator of intelligence at work.

Turing himself took forward the development of this idea. Chess-playing ability quickly became accepted as another clear test of intelligence. In the 1940s, both Turing and Claude Shannon (the founder of the field we now know as *information theory*) published papers on the mechanics of a theoretical chess-playing computer. Intensive work in this area followed, until 1958, when Allen Newell, Herbert Simon and Cliff Shaw published 'Chess-playing programs and the problem of complexity', in which they stated:

> Chess is the intellectual game par excellence ... It pits two intellects against each other in a situation so complex that neither can hope to understand it completely ... If one could devise a successful chess machine, one would seem to have penetrated the core of human intellectual endeavour.

Source: Newell et al. (1958)

Although the authors might not have realised it, these insights were to define much of the programme of Symbolic AI for the next forty years.

Exercise 1.10

Earlier, I claimed that the key concepts of Symbolic AI were *representation* and *search*. We'll discuss these concepts exhaustively in Block 2, but for now how do you think that a chess-playing computer might be based on representation and search?

Discussion ....

Think about chess for a moment. Even if you are not a player, you know that there is a *board* of 64 squares, on which are *pieces*, in certain *positions* which change from move to move. It seems clear that if a computer is to play chess at all, it must work with some kind of *model* or *representation* of the changing state of the board as the game proceeds from move to move, as the patterns of the pieces shift, and as pieces are taken. You can also see that at any point in the game when it is the machine's move, the program will have to choose the best move to make in the circumstances. This means *searching* for, and selecting, the best move from among all the legal alternatives at each point.

In his early paper, Shannon had seen exactly this. He envisaged that building a chess-playing program was a three-part problem:

1   making a representation of the state of the board that could be stored in a computer;

2   finding a search strategy that will find the best move;

3   translating this search strategy into a series of instructions that the computer can carry out.

The idea of chess-playing as a key indicator of intelligent thought, realised through representation and search, became cemented into place as a core strategy of the Symbolic AI project. We'll examine the adequacy, the successes and failures of approaches based on representation and search in Block 2.

You'll recall that in 'Computing machinery and intelligence' Turing begins with the question 'Can machines think?'. This in turn implies two preliminary questions: 'What is a machine?' and 'What is thinking?'. We've now looked at Turing's and other AI pioneers' answers to the second of these questions – thinking is essentially something that we can recognise externally through behavioural investigations like the Turing Test; internally it relates to problem-solving procedures based on representation and search.

Whether this is altogether a satisfactory account of thinking and intelligence is a question we will address throughout the course. I'll come back to it briefly in the next section and Block 3 will present alternative accounts of intelligence. Let's now consider Turing's answer to the first question: 'What is a machine?'.

SAQ 1.7

Try to sum up what Turing meant by a 'machine' in his paper 'Computing machinery and intelligence'. Refer back to the paper if you need to.

ANSWER..

Turing leaves us in no doubt that by 'machine' he means the digital computer. For Turing, a digital computer is a device with a *store*, an *executive unit* and a *control*. The store will contain a 'book of rules' telling the computer exactly what to do next at each step. It can also be used as a scratchpad for storing data and intermediate results. Computers are *discrete state machines* in that the machine moves through a series of states, the next state being determined unambiguously by the current state and the input the control unit is receiving. The states are discrete because there is no ambiguity or middle ground between one state or another – the machine is either in state 1 or state 2: it cannot ever be in state 1/2. Finally, digital computers are *universal machines*. They can mimic any discrete state machine simply by adding a new book of rules to the store.

If we substitute the more up-to-date terms 'memory' for 'store', 'CPU' for 'executive unit', and 'program' for 'book of rules', we have the modern computer. This is the machine that the founding fathers of Symbolic AI believed could be programmed to think. The digital computer was at the heart of their project from the start.

4.2 | Cybernetics and Symbolic AI

Now is a good time to pause for a moment. I want to sum up what I hope you've learned about the two projects: Cybernetics and Symbolic AI.

Exercise 1.11

Write a few notes summarising what you think are the key differences between Cybernetics and Symbolic AI. I'll present a full answer below, so don't go into too much detail here.

Discussion ....

The key differences seem to me to have been that the Cybernetics movement is a multidisciplinary study of control and response in a changing environment, centring mainly on the reality of nervous systems and feedback. By contrast, AI is an investigation of human intelligence as a form of computation, and is based on principles of representation and search.

Cybernetics was an intellectual movement that was inspired by questions about how animals and humans maintained equilibrium within, and responded appropriately to, their ever-changing environment. From the start it was a multidisciplinary movement and less clearly defined than Symbolic AI. However, I think one can safely say that the thinking of the cyberneticists centred on the following ideas:

▶ *Computers*. Thinkers like Wiener were, of course, aware of the digital computer, and computing of some kind was central to their project. However, Cybernetics originated before digital machines had made a real impact, and cyberneticists tended to be agnostic about the kind of computers they needed. Cybernetic systems like Ashby's Homeostat, for instance, were based on analogue computation.

▶ *Nervous systems*. Cyberneticists were particularly interested in human and animal nervous systems. They saw these as the key to intelligence, but were not dogmatic about how the principles of nervous systems could be replicated in actual machines.

▶ *Feedback and other mechanisms*. You've already learned that Cybernetics saw abstract mechanisms such as feedback as the key to intelligent behaviour.

▶ *Environment and embodiment*. For the cyberneticists, the response of an animal or a machine to what was going on in the *environment* around it was of central interest. Feedback from, and correct response to, stimuli received from the world around devices such as the anti-aircraft predictor were fundamental. Cybernetic machines, like animal bodies, were not intended to be remote from the world around them, but in constant interaction with it.

▶ *Indicators of intelligence.* Cyberneticists were not especially interested in intelligence in the human sense. They tended to focus on characteristics that both humans and animals had in common, such as activity and purposeful behaviour.

As we've seen, Symbolic AI was – and is – more narrowly focused. These are some of its main characteristics, in my view. Note the contrasts with Cybernetics.

▶ *Computers.* All Symbolic AI research took the electronic digital computer, as it was understood by Turing, as its starting point and principal tool. There was some early interest in nervous systems among the Dartmouth scientists and others. However, for reasons I'll mention later, this soon fell by the wayside.

▶ *Intelligence as computation.* As for Hobbes, it seemed obvious to the founders of Symbolic AI that intelligence, thinking, was a form of computation, a manipulation of symbols. Mechanisms like feedback from the environment played little if any part in their theories.

▶ *Representation* and *search.* So, if thinking was a form of symbol manipulation that could be imitated on a digital computer, then the way to tackle any problem involving thinking was to *represent* the problem in some symbolic form capable of being programmed into a computer and then manipulate the symbols in an appropriate way. As we've seen, this generally involved some kind of *search.*

▶ *Indicators of intelligence.* Although Symbolic AI researchers may have had a passing interest in animal intelligence, their focus was overwhelmingly on human intelligence of the most abstract kind. Key tests were the Turing Test and the ability to play board games, especially chess.

The contrast between these two radically different models can be summed up in the diagrams in Figure 1.10.

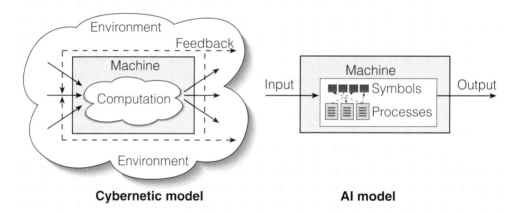

Cybernetic model   **AI model**

Figure 1.10   Cybernetic and Symbolic AI models

For Symbolic AI, then, the digital computer is king. But this is not just because it is the ideal tool. The fathers of Symbolic AI had a much more radical idea in mind. It was this: that at some deep level, the human brain and interpreted automatic formal devices such as the digital computer are *equivalent* systems. The fact that they are realised in different kinds of materials – protoplasm and silicon – is irrelevant. In all ways that matter, they are exactly the *same* system. Intelligence *is* computation.

This is an exceptionally bold claim; but now is not the time to ask how true it is. We'll return to this point in Block 6. Let's just note that the digital computer is the tool with which every researcher in artificial intelligence, whether they work inside the Symbolic AI tradition or not, now works.

4.3 Artificial intelligence – the quest

The goal of artificial intelligence is to build intelligent systems. So far, we've considered what intelligence might be and how we might recognise an intelligent system when we see one. But now let's try to unpick the real nature of the quest for artificial intelligence a bit further. When we say we want to build intelligent systems, what are we really trying to achieve?

You might recall a question I posed earlier about the attitude of the automata builders of the 18th century to their creations. I asked whether Vaucanson, for example, might have imagined his duck was to some degree truly a living thing, rather than just a clever *simulacrum* of a real water fowl. If it could be made into a much, much more accurate simulacrum could it become, in some way, the real living thing?

This is a very difficult question. But it is directly relevant to the quest for artificial intelligence. What are we *really* trying to achieve when we build intelligent computer systems? There are two distinct possibilities:

1   We are trying to build practical systems that will do certain clever things. This may give us certain insights into the human mental processes that underlie intelligent behaviour along the way, but no more than that. Such systems are not intended to be accurate imitations of mental processes. Moreover, each simulation might be quite narrow in scope – good at playing chess, say, but useless at checkers, language or medical diagnosis.

2   We are trying to build systems that faithfully copy mental processes. If that is our aim then the question we started with – Could the imitation ever become the reality? – becomes pertinent. Suppose we could very precisely reproduce mental process on a computer; might we end up with something that is genuinely intelligent, is aware, has a *mind*? Something like you and me?

In 1980, the philosopher John Searle proposed the terms **weak artificial intelligence** and **strong artificial intelligence** to describe exactly these two possibilities. Here is a brief outline of his ideas.

Weak artificial intelligence

This is possibility 1 above. Weak artificial intelligence is a research programme that attempts to throw some light on human mental processes and to build practical, working systems that will do clever things and will serve as useful tools. In Searle's words:

> According to weak [artificial intelligence], the principal value of the computer in the study of the mind is that it gives us a very powerful tool. For example, it enables us to formulate and test hypotheses in a more rigorous and precise fashion.

Source: Searle (1980)

But let me stress again that weak artificial intelligence is an intensely practical, engineering discipline. The aim is to build computer systems with recognisable, if limited, intelligent behaviour.

Strong artificial intelligence

Strong artificial intelligence is summed up in possibility 2. The goal is intelligently behaving computers, as before. But for strong artificial intelligence there is more to it than that. Searle writes:

> ... according to strong [artificial intelligence], the computer is not merely a tool in the study of the mind; rather, the appropriately programmed computer really is a mind.

Source: Searle (1980)

If, as I suggested above, at some level, the human brain and the digital computer are *equivalent* systems, then surely this is a possibility? Symbolic AI pioneers like Turing and McCarthy certainly believed in the possibility of strong artificial intelligence. These days it is hard to find researchers who will openly admit to believing in it. Our course is overwhelmingly concerned with strategies and techniques that would be called weak artificial intelligence. However, whether researchers want to acknowledge it or not, strong artificial intelligence is a prospect that always remains in the corner of our eyes. We will return to the question in Block 6.

SAQ 1.8

Sum up what you understand by the terms *weak artificial intelligence* and *strong artificial intelligence*.

ANSWER..

Weak artificial intelligence is a practical programme that aims to build computer systems that have intelligent behaviour, but are not necessarily based on human mental processes. Such systems are likely to be quite narrow in their behavioural scope. Weak artificial intelligence can also be a tool for psychological investigations of these processes.

Strong artificial intelligence looks to imitate human mental processes with the aim of building computer systems that are intelligent in the same way as humans, and may even be sentient in the way that humans are.

Weak or strong, artificial intelligence and the computer are inextricably bound together. Stripping away irrelevant details, such as what software it runs, what company makes it, what processor it uses and how much memory it has, and so on, what exactly *is* a digital computer?

5 Computers

5.1 The digital computer

Turing can rightly be called the founding father of computer technology. It was his pioneering mathematical work before the Second World War, and the practical engineering he and his colleagues carried out at Bletchley Park, that led to the machines that now sit on nearly every desk. We take them so much for granted now that it is worth making a small effort to restate what, in essence, a computer *is* and what it *does*, and to recall what the concept 'computer' meant to Turing.

The AI theorist John Haugeland has called the computer an *interpreted automatic formal system*. Since the exact nature of this tool at the heart of Symbolic AI (and artificial intelligence generally) is bound to influence crucially the content and direction of the whole endeavour, we need to consider what he means. Let's examine Haugeland's definition by working from the end backwards, so to speak, by starting with the notion of a formal system.

The argument I'm summarising here is taken from John Haugeland's book *Artificial Intelligence: The very idea* (1985).

Formal systems

The computer is an interpreted automatic formal system. Therefore, it must be, first of all, a formal system. Many board games are formal systems too; so let's define such systems using the game of chess as an example. A formal system comprises three components:

1   A set of **tokens**. These tokens may be of one **token-type** only, or of several different types. In chess, for instance, the tokens are the chess pieces: 32 of them, of six types. Tokens may be simple or complex, but we don't need to discuss this here.

2   A **starting state**. This is a certain disposition of tokens with which the system is set up at the beginning of play. In chess, as you know, the start position looks like Figure 1.11.

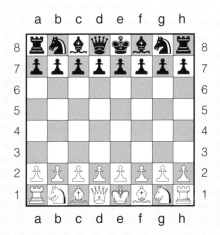

Figure 1.11   Chess starting state

3   From this starting state, the tokens can be manipulated according to a set of **rules**. Each rule allows the system to move into a new state. In chess the rules stipulate how pieces can be moved legally around the board, the constraints on these movements, how pieces are captured, and so on. These rules can be quite complex. For example, a bishop can move any number of squares diagonally forwards or backwards from its current position, with the constraint that it cannot move onto a square occupied by a piece of its own colour, or over a square occupied by a piece of any colour. If any piece moves to a square occupied by a piece of the opposing colour, then that piece is said to be *captured* and is removed from the board. The rules of other board games may be simpler, but they are in exactly the same spirit.

Applying a rule legally moves the system into a new state. In chess these states are the board positions, as in Figure 1.12. Some of these positions may be specially designated as *winning positions*, but although this adds interest and excitement to games, it is not an essential feature of a formal system.

Figure 1.12   A chess state during play

These three properties are sufficient to define a formal system fully. But formal systems have several important features that we need to be clear about.

▶   First of all, they are **discrete**. What does this mean? Just this: for a formal system to work at all it must be possible to *read* and *write* tokens successfully. In our chess example, reading a token means *recognising* a particular piece, what type it is and what position it is in, etc.; writing a token means *moving* it to a new position. Formal systems must have a *positive*, *reliable* method of reading and writing. Here, positive and reliable have special meanings:

positive means that a token must be read and written with *absolute success*. This might sound a bit enigmatic, but it is simply the point Turing was making in the passage you considered in SAQ 1.7. A token is either recognised or it is not recognised; it is either written to a certain place, or it is not written to that place. There can be no half measures, no fractions, no degrees of uncertainty. This becomes clearer if we consider our chess example again. A knight in a cheap chess set may be a slightly different shape from the other knights; never mind – it is still a knight and not a bishop or a pawn. The knight may not be quite at the centre of square a4, it may even be close to one of the edges: that doesn't matter; it is still on a4, without qualification or doubt. If a piece is precisely on the border between two squares then the system *must* make a decision as to which of the two it is actually on. It cannot settle for an indeterminate answer, like 'halfway between a4 and b4'. It must decide on either a4 or b4. If it cannot make such a decision, it must make no decision.

reliable just means that the system must have an extremely high likelihood of success in reading and writing tokens. Of course, absolute perfection cannot be guaranteed, but the chances of success must be very high.

A simpler example might help. Haugeland asks us to consider a multi-position switch – let's say it's a three-position rocker switch, the positions being On, Off and Auto. The system has to be able to read the position of the switch. Quite likely, each time it is in a certain position its precise angle may be minutely different. But this doesn't matter: the switch must be read as *either* Off *or* On *or* Auto – it can never be some combination of, or compromise between, these. Similarly, when the switch is read as being at a certain position, a particular circuit must be opened or closed. A circuit can't be half opened or, say, the On and the Auto circuits both opened together. It's one or the other, all or nothing. It is a discrete system.

▶ Purely formal systems have the property of **medium-independence**. It does not matter what the tokens are made of, or how the system is realised physically. Again, our chess example is useful here. Of course, chess pieces can be made of wood, plastic, ivory, steel, or whatever. Chess has even been played with living people as pieces. This doesn't affect the nature of the game at all. Stretching the imagination a bit, one could play chess with ships at sea, or with each individual square of the board in a different county, or (given a super-technology) with an assembly of asteroids. As you know, chess can be played by computers, with no physical board or pieces at all. All that matters is that the tokens can be read and written, the 64 board positions are identifiable and writeable, and the rules. You can see echoes here of the question I posed earlier about Hobbes' view of intelligence as computation with symbols.

▶ Given this, it follows that the formal system is **self-contained** – a closed world. In chess, it doesn't matter who is playing, where they are playing, what the weather is like, and so on. The only issues that are relevant are the positions of the tokens and the legality of each move, within the rules of the game. Even more importantly, the tokens themselves have no intrinsic *meaning*. It doesn't matter whether the knight token is shaped like a horse, or a piece of broccoli, or (as in computer chess) is just a pattern of voltages. The knight token is just that – a token. The only *meaning* a token has is the purely formal meaning that comes from what the rules allow one to do with it.

▶ A formal system must be **finitely playable**. Again, this idea needs to be spelled out. A minimum definition of a finitely playable formal system is that in any state of the system a finite player must be able to:

— deduce whether every possible move is legal or not;

— find at least one legal move, or be certain that there are none.

Unfortunately, this doesn't take us much further forward. What is a finite player? Well, a useful definition from our point of view is this: for every state of the system, a finite player must be capable of deciding on each of the two points above by means of an **algorithm**.

I assume most of you know what an algorithm is already. If you want, just check your understanding against mine with the following brief question.

SAQ 1.9

What is an algorithm?

ANSWER...

I expect most of you wrote something along the lines of 'a set of steps for arriving at a certain result'. You may have added that after each step, the next step is fully obvious, with no alternatives. This is quite right, but there are two other points to add. First of all, an algorithm is **infallible**: it is *guaranteed* to provide the expected result, provided it is followed correctly. Secondly, an algorithm must be **finite**: it must be able to reach the result in a finite number of steps (although the number of steps may be as large as you like).

Now let's expand our discussion and look at automatic formal systems.

Automatic formal systems

As I expect you've guessed, an **automatic formal system** is simply one that works by itself, without any outside intervention. This does mean that the system requires another component, a *referee* that enforces the rules. In the case of chess, this means ensuring that players don't move out of turn, setting up the start position correctly, monitoring the legality of moves, and so on. Of course, most chess players will abide by these rules anyway; although at the highest levels of human play, there are referees. Recall the extract from Turing's paper 'Computing machinery and intelligence' – the referee function we're talking about here is exactly what Turing meant by the control unit. Its job is to ensure the system's algorithms are followed correctly.

For automatic formal systems, then, the Principle of Automation applies:

Principle of Automation

Whenever the legal moves of a formal system are fully determined by algorithms, then that system can be automated.

Source: Haugeland, *Artificial Intelligence: The very idea* (1985)

A serious problem arises in automatic formal systems. At each state of the system the algorithm must by itself find a legal move (or decide that no move is possible). However, in many formal systems, for any particular state there is often a large number of moves, all perfectly legal, to choose from. Such systems are known as **non-deterministic**, as opposed to **deterministic systems**, where only one legal move is available in each state (and which would thus make absolutely rotten games). Chess is a perfect example of a non-deterministic formal system. Glance back at Figure 1.12. Assuming it is white's turn to move, how many legal moves are available? Don't bother to count them yourself; I've done it for you. Unless I've miscounted, an automated system playing white would have to choose between 51 legal moves at that point. If you are a chess player yourself, you'll be able to see straight away that many of them are immediately suicidal, others merely pointless. But which is the *best* move, and how is it to be selected?

A very brief answer to this question is that the selection algorithm must incorporate **heuristics** for choosing the best move. But I'm going to leave the matter there for the time being. The question of heuristics, what they are and how they work, will come up in Block 2, where we'll discuss them in detail.

A heuristic means, roughly, 'a rule of thumb' or 'a guide in the investigation or solution of a problem'.

Interpreted automatic formal systems

Finally, the matter of Haugeland's point about interpretation. Computers are *interpreted* automatic formal systems. So what does 'interpretation' mean here?

Interpretation is concerned with the whole question of *meaning*, and meaning is the province of the study known as **semantics**. Questions of semantics too often lead one into a philosophical morass that I want to step gingerly around. Let's start with our chess example again. Chess is a formal system. Earlier I claimed that in formal systems the tokens have no intrinsic meaning. But this claim needs to be examined a bit more closely.

SAQ 1.10

If, say, the knight token in the formal system of chess has any meaning at all, what is it and where does it come from?

ANSWER...

I think this question may be easier to answer than it was to phrase. The *only* meaning the knight token has comes from *what the rules allow us to do with it*. The knight token is the one that can be moved two squares up (or back) and then one square to the left or right, or one square up (or back) and then two squares to the left or right.

This is why it's irrelevant whether the knight token is made of plastic or of plutonium, or is shaped like a beetle or like Batman. The only meaning it has within the formal system is the characteristic moves it is allowed to make. We can call this sort of meaning the **operational semantics** of the token.

However, the fact that the tokens of a formal system have this kind of semantics doesn't necessarily mean that such systems are interpreted systems. In interpreted systems, the tokens have another meaning: they *stand for*, they *refer to*, things in the world outside the system. Chess is a formal system. It is a formal system that can be automated. But it is not an interpreted formal system. The tokens have no meaning outside the rules of the game. So let's leave chess for a moment and work with another example.

In interpreted systems, the meaning of a token is the thing, or things, in the world that it refers to. They cease to be mere tokens and become **symbols**, standing for real things. In the jargon, they have a **denotational semantics**. To take another example, again suggested by Haugeland, suppose we have a system comprising

1 fourteen tokens, the letters a through to n;

2 various start states consisting of strings of tokens;

3 a set of rules, one for each start state, each of which leads to the addition of one or more tokens to the end of the start state. After a single move the system halts.

A couple of examples of the system in action will be enough.

Table 1.1

Start state	New state after move
aka	aka ce
bkfnb	bkfnb b
cgmami	cgmami egj

At the moment this looks like a purely formal system, and a pretty pointless one too. But now suppose that each of the various tokens *stands for* one of the numbers 0 through to 9, or for one of the arithmetic operators +, −, * and / (that is, add, subtract, multiply, divide). For instance, a → 7, b → 3, k → +, and so on. Substituting objects for the tokens, then, an **interpretation** of the system makes might look like this:

Table 1.2

Start state	New state after move
7 + 7	7 + 7 14
3 + 6 / 3	3 + 6 / 3 3

... and so on. Our old friend, school arithmetic. However, if you try the following straightforward interpretation:

a → +   h → 3

b → −   i → 4

c → *   j → 5

d → /   k → 6

e → 0   l → 7

f → 1   m → 8

g → 2   n → 9

you get the following nonsensical result:

Table 1.3

Start state	New state after move
+ 6 +	+ 6 + *0
− 6 1 9 −	− 6 1 9 − −
* 2 8 + 8 4	* 2 8 + 8 4 025

Clearly, only one set of denotations, one **mapping** of tokens to numbers, will produce the standard arithmetical system from our examples in Table 1.1. But which one? Don't bother to try and work it out. There are over 87 billion ways to ascribe fourteen symbols to fourteen numbers and signs. The right interpretation in this case is:

a → 7   h → 9

b → 3   i → 5

c → 1   j → 0

d → 8   k → +

e → 4   l → −

f → 6   m → *

g → 2   n → /

which you can see will give us correct arithmetical expressions and results for the examples in Table 1.1. So here is an example of an interpreted formal system. And, as we all know, such systems can be automated. Our pocket calculators tell us so.

That's almost as far as I want to go here. But one final point is important, though. Consider this mapping:

a → 0	h → 7
b → 1	i → 8
c → 2	j → 9
d → 3	k → +
e → 4	l → −
f → 5	m → *
g → 6	n → /

If we then lay out our original examples according to this interpretation, we get:

Table 1.4

Start state	New state after move
0 + 0	0 + 0 24
1 + 5 / 1	1 + 5 / 1 1
26 * 0 * 8	26 * 0 * 8 469

This is a different kind of nonsense to that of Table 1.2. The arithmetical expressions in the left-hand column are all quite valid, unlike the jumble of symbols we got in Table 1.2. However, the results we get after making the move are just plain wrong. The interpretation produces statements that are quite correctly arranged but are simply untrue. So my final point about interpreted formal systems is this: their rules must be designed to be **truth-preserving**. Every rule that operates on a certain state of the system that is true under a certain interpretation should produce a new state that is also true under that interpretation. I know you'll want to take my word for it, but if you like you can verify that the system I've presented is truth-preserving under the interpretation I offered.

Exercise 1.12

This discussion all started with my proposal that digital computers are interpreted automatic formal systems, comprising tokens, rules and so on. Write a few notes relating what you know of how digital computers fit into these definitions.

Discussion ....

It should be fairly easy to state how the concept of the digital computer fits in with these definitions. Considering the computer running a program as a formal system:

1   The *tokens* are the various *data structures* of the program, distributed across the memory of the machine. These data structures may just be individual bits, or variables, or complex structures such as arrays or objects (or arrays of objects, and so on).

2   The *start state* is the initialisation of these data structures to their starting values, or defaults. The control unit of the computer also sets the program counter to the first instruction in the program.

3   The *rules* are embodied in the *program*, a finite algorithm that specifies exactly how the tokens are to be read and written, and in what order these read/write operations are to take place.

We should note that the computer has all the other properties of a purely formal system:

4   It is *discrete*, because the digital nature of the device means that ultimately it deals only in 1s and 0s, which must be read and written reliably, with absolute success, as 1s and 0s, with no intermediate values allowed.

5   It is *medium-independent*. This may seem a bit more perplexing, because we are so used to the idea of computers as silicon-based, electronic devices. However, it is only for reasons of speed, size and practicality that they are so. There is no theoretical reason why a digital computer might not be constructed out of sealing wax or glass beads. Babbage's analytical engine and the abacus are, in their way, computers too.

6   We know that computers are *finitely playable*, as the programs they run are, without exception, algorithmic.

Now, obviously a computer is an *automatic formal system*, as it runs on its own. The referee function is built into the CPU, ensuring the correct starting point of the program and that the algorithm specified in the program is executed in the correct order. The algorithmic nature of the program ensures that each step can be identified positively and reliably.

Finally, a computer is an *interpreted* system. Computers are tools that we use for our own real-world purposes. What they do, and the results they produce, have a meaning for us. The data inside programs stand for things of interest to us in the world outside the program.

To grasp this last point a little more clearly, consider a meteorological program simulating some portion of the Earth's atmosphere. The program is running on a supercomputer and is being used for weather prediction. Now let's say that at location F734CD61 in the computer's memory is a variable containing a certain value. As far as the machine is concerned this is just a token, and at some point in the execution of the program it is required to write a new value into this slot. However, for the human builders and users of the system the token at F734CD61 has a *meaning*. It refers to a measurement of atmospheric pressure at a certain spot on the Earth's surface; the new value that is written for the token stands for the pressure to be expected at that spot at a certain time in the future. Although the machine treats the token purely formally, we interpret it: it has been given a human meaning.

These interpreted automatic formal systems, these computers, are a dominant technology of our time. They are clearly immensely capable tools. Given their central role in the artificial intelligence project, it's time to give a little thought to what they can do. More importantly, though, are there things they can't do?

5.2   What computers can do

We're all aware in some way or another what computers are capable of. They play three-dimensional games, process words, control satellites and washing machines, make calculations, display movies, manipulate photographic images, and so on. Their powers seem endless.

It would be futile to multiply examples. In this section, I want to consider just two aspects of the digital computer's abilities that are, at the same time, rather more abstract than these concrete examples, and more relevant to our focus: artificial intelligence. They are the power of the digital computer to:

1   work with *models* of real-world systems; and

2   solve a special class of problems called *optimisation problems*.

Let's start with the first of these.

Models

Earlier, I referred to the fact that computers manipulate tokens in the form of bits, variables and complex data structures. And, as I suggested, to play chess the computer must work with some representation of the state of the board as it changes from move to move. Interpreted computer systems, whatever their purpose, all contain representations of this kind. Many computer systems are, of course, imitations in this sense: they are what we daily refer to as **models**.

SAQ 1.11

Jot down your own definition of the term *model*. What is a computer model?

ANSWER..

I thought the best way of putting it is that a model is a *simplified picture of reality*. It may be helpful here to think of the sort of models that children like to build. A plastic model of a battleship will reproduce the ship's main structures – guns, decks, hull, superstructure, and so on – but will probably leave out most of the internal workings. It certainly will not include details that are too small to matter, such as the individual cogs of a windlass, or are considered irrelevant, such as flecks of rust on the hull, or a seagull sitting on the stern.

A computer model is obviously more abstract than this, but is essentially the same idea. It is a representation on a computer of some aspect of reality. Since even the tiniest segments of the real world are immensely more complex than anything that could possibly be represented exactly on any known – or foreseeable – computer, models are always simplifications.

But a model of some system found in the world is not necessarily one kind of thing. Broadly speaking, there are three possibilities:

1   a **simulation** of a natural system is a model that captures the functional connections between inputs and outputs of the system;

2   a **replication** of a natural system is a model that captures the functional connections between inputs and outputs of the system and is based on processes that are the same as, or similar to, those of the real-world system;

3   an **emulation** of a natural system is a model that captures the functional connections between inputs and outputs of the system, based on processes that are the same as, or similar to, those of the natural system, and in the same materials as the natural system.

In other words, a *simulation* provides the correct output for every input that is given to it, but does it using processes that may be quite unlike those of the system it is a model of. A *replication* arrives at correct outputs using procedures that model the actual processes of the real-world system itself. As for emulations, not only do they produce correct outputs from replications of the processes of the real-world system, the model is made from the same physical substances as that system. If this still seems a bit unclear, it may be helpful to consider a few examples.

Exercise 1.13

This is quite a challenging question, but try to think of at least one example of each of the three kinds of model above. Your examples don't necessarily have to be computer models.

Discussion ....

Simulation. A good example of a simulation might be an electronic calculator. It mimics the processes by which we do arithmetic, in that it captures the connection between a certain input, say 2 + 2, and the output (4) that a human would give if presented with this sum. However, you are well aware that the actual processes the computer uses are based on binary arithmetic, which are nothing like the models we would base our own calculations on. The kinds of automata we looked at earlier are also examples of simulations. In the case of such artefacts, the old maxim, 'it walks like a duck, it quacks like a duck, then by God it is a duck!' is simply untrue: they produce duck-like responses to certain stimuli, but internally they don't even faintly resemble ducks.

Replication. You might have found it harder to come up with an example of a replication. Many computer models are based on mathematical abstractions that are nothing like the phenomena they are claiming to represent – so they are simulations. However, other kinds of models do come closer to the phenomena they represent. Models of the Earth's atmosphere, for instance, used by meteorologists for weather prediction, are usually based on fairly explicit representations of the interaction of the air with the land, the oceans and the energy of the sun, so factors such as pressure, temperature, humidity, wind speed, along with the laws that relate them, are generally represented explicitly. In General Circulation Models, for example, the Earth's surface is partitioned into a rectangular grid, with each rectangle the base of a column, extending from the surface to high in the atmosphere. Each column is divided into layers, thus splitting the whole atmosphere into a network of three-dimensional boxes. In each box the temperature, pressure, humidity, wind speed and direction, and other features are recorded. Although it is obviously not possible, with any conceivable computer, to model every single particle of air, such models do attempt to represent the natural phenomena they are based on. A chess-playing computer program is also a good example of a replication: pieces, their positions on the board, moves and constraints are all represented explicitly in the model.

Emulation. In the early 1950s Stanley L. Miller, working at the University of Chicago, conducted an experiment that attempted to clarify what chemical reactions had occurred on the primitive Earth. He created a model of the Earth's oceans by heating water in a flask and forcing water vapour to circulate through the apparatus. The flask also contained a model of the Earth's early atmosphere, consisting of methane, ammonia, hydrogen and the circulating water vapour. Miller then passed a continuous electrical discharge (a model of lightning) through the flask, causing the gases to interact. Water-soluble products of those reactions then passed through a condenser and dissolved in the model ocean. The experiment yielded several amino acids, the building blocks of proteins. Miller's model used the actual chemical constituents that may have existed on the early Earth, and so is an example of an emulation.

SAQ 1.12

Returning to Vaucanson's Duck for the last time, do you think it was an emulation, a simulation or a replication?

ANSWER...

A tricky question! To express this in the vocabulary I've just developed, we know that the duck could not have been an *emulation* (since it was made of metal and not protoplasm). But it's not clear to what extent it was just a *simulation* (just a lifelike imitation), and to what extent a *replication* (copying the inner workings of a real duck). And could a replication, in some way, approach the real living thing?

It seems pretty clear that computer models can never be emulations, where it is crucial that the model is built out of the same kinds of physical substance as the real-world system. Pretty well all the models we discuss in this course are attempts at replications of one form or another. To what extent realistic models of intelligence can be genuine replications rather than just simulations is a knotty problem. Defenders of strong artificial intelligence would argue that perfect replications are theoretically possible and that these replications would *be intelligent* – would *be minds*. Most researchers would probably deny this. We'll leave the problem for now and return to it in Block 6.

It's reasonable to think of typical computer replications as large, intricate things. To take our chess example again, the representation of the board and the rules that manipulate it will be a single, very complex model, with many interlocking features. However, one kind of model – one which will turn up a lot in the course – is rather different. It is a model in which *many* smaller, simple models – usually they are all the same model – are put together and made to interact with one another. There are lots of names for this kind of system. I'll refer to it as a **distributed interactive system**, or simply a **complex system**. To clarify this idea and to prepare for later practical work, try the following experiment.

Computer Exercise 1.1

In this exercise you will set up a simple interactive system, look at its properties and draw some general conclusions. Go to the course DVD, locate Computer Exercise 1.1 and follow the instructions.

Now let's move on and consider the second feature of computer abilities.

Optimisation problems

In general terms an **optimisation problem** is just one in which the task is to find the *best* possible solution from among a number of alternatives. Seen in these abstract terms, a huge proportion of the problems we look to computers to solve for us are optimisation problems. You'll recall from our earlier discussion that Turing and the Symbolic AI trail-blazers of the Dartmouth conference saw certain kinds of intelligent thought as a process of search, in which the best solution is selected from all the alternatives. If they were right, artificial intelligence is a set of optimisation problems too.

In mathematics, an optimisation problem is one in which the task is to find the point, or points, at which a function reaches its maximum (or minimum) value, generally subject to some constraints. To take an extremely simple example, suppose we want to find the maximum area of a rectangle with a perimeter of no more that 16 cm. We can formulate this as an optimisation problem, as follows:

> Assuming the rectangle has sides x and y, the function $f(x,y)$ we are optimising is $x * y$ (since the area of a rectangle is obtained by multiplying the lengths of its sides). The problem is to find values of x and y that give the maximum value for $f(x,y)$. The constraint is that $2x + 2y \leq 16$.

This example may seem quite trivial, but such problems can prove hideously tough computationally.

In computing, however, optimisation problems are generally ones in which the search is for the best solutions from among a number of possibilities. The most frequently occurring of these are **combinatorial optimisation problems** (COPs), where, as the name suggests, the task is to find the best *combination* of discrete values from some given set. The classic COP – familiar to every computer scientist – is the *Travelling Salesman Problem* (TSP), probably the most commonly used example in computing courses anywhere. The TSP is not a realistic problem, but it is popular among teachers of Computer Science because it is so simple to state and to visualise. Here is a brief description of it – if you know about it already, by all means skip the next couple of paragraphs.

A salesperson is required to visit N cities, each city being a certain distance from the others, for example as in the following grid, showing a five-city TSP.

Table 1.5

	Exeter	Bristol	Manchester	Leeds	London
Exeter	X	74	236	278	173
Bristol	74	X	165	207	119
Manchester	236	165	X	43	198
Leeds	278	207	43	X	195
London	173	119	198	195	X

Notice that in this example the grid is symmetrical, but it need not be: a different route could be used to get from Manchester to London, say, from the route from London to Manchester.

The task is simple: find the order in which to visit all five cities that gives the *shortest* round trip, or *tour*. This looks easy enough to achieve, on the face of it – just try every combination until you find the best one. But this approach, known as *brute force*, very rapidly becomes impractical: our example has five cities, and there are 120 possible combinations of this basic set. However, if the salesperson has to visit ten cities, there are 3,628,800 tours; for fifteen cities, 1,307,674,368,000; for twenty cities the number of tours is roughly 2.43×10^{18}. As the number of cities increases, it rapidly becomes impossible for any actual or imaginable computer to handle the number of combinations involved, using the brute-force approach – it would just take too long. The brute-force strategy entails what is termed a **combinatorial explosion**. The TSP is a problem that is known in computational complexity theory as *NP-hard*. Since this is not a course in the theory of computation, all we need say about this is that NP-hard problems are ones in which there is no known algorithm for solving them in any realistic period of time (although such algorithms may exist).

SAQ 1.13

I mentioned above that optimisation problems are sometimes constrained. Think of one or more possible constraints on the TSP.

ANSWER...

One obvious constraint is that the salesperson should never visit the same city twice. We might find that there were other constraints, such as it being impossible to move from one city (say Manchester) to another (say Leeds) for practical reasons, such as absence of suitable transport, company rules, etc.

As we said above, the TSP is not a problem of any practical importance in itself. But it has all the features of a vast set of problems that *are* of major importance in computing, engineering and science. Here are two examples:

▶ *Circuit board drilling.* In the manufacture of printed circuit boards, computer-controlled machines drill holes and insert parts into the boards. The problem is to plot a route for the tool to travel across the board that will minimise machine time and tooling costs.

▶ *Protein folding.* Proteins are made up of chains of amino acids, which are transcribed from ribonucleic acid (RNA) as a linear sequence. After transcription, the sequence rapidly folds up into a three-dimensional structure which is generally the most energy-conservative one possible. The problem is to predict, for any given protein, what that 3-D structure will be, from among all the possible formations its sequence can fold into.

SAQ 1.14

Note down one or two other examples of optimisation problems you've heard of.

ANSWER...

All sorts of answers are possible. Most planning and scheduling problems, for example, are optimisation problems. Scheduling of aircraft flights, working out the order in which to remove the supports on a completed structure such as a bridge, and planning the layout of a factory floor are all good examples. Even planning the best way to get to work in the morning, a classic example of an artificial intelligence problem, is a matter of optimisation.

Because they are so important, many computational strategies have been developed to tackle COPs. You've probably come across some of them yourself, but there's no need to look at any of them here. Instead, I just want to make two important general points about optimisation problems:

1   For every TSP, there may be one, and only one, *best* solution. But unless we can use brute force, which for larger problems we just can't do, then it may simply not be possible to find that one, best solution. We may have to be satisfied with merely *very good* solutions.

2   Given that in practice it is very difficult to find the best, or even good, solutions by brute force, search strategies have to be supplemented in some way. Clever short cuts in the search process have to be found. These are the *heuristics* I mentioned. For Symbolic AI thinkers, heuristics are where the intelligence in artificial intelligence comes in.

You'll find these two points reinforced throughout Blocks 2 and 3.

5.3 | What computers can't do?

So we've noted some of the apparently boundless applications of the digital computer and looked at two of its key abilities. But are there things that computers simply *aren't* capable of *in principle*? This is a much more difficult question than it appears at first sight. What I really mean to ask is this: are there things relevant to intelligent behaviour that computers, because of their very nature, simply can't do?

Exercise 1.14

Consider this question for a few minutes. Do you think there are limitations on computers which mean that they are incapable of intelligence in principle? What might they be? Jot down a few notes about this.

Discussion ....

It's tempting to offer quite facile answers such as 'a computer couldn't make a cup of tea'. But actually, if it was operating a suitable robot, making a cup of tea might just be the kind of thing a computer *could* do. I can't see why not. You might have wanted to say, 'well, a computer couldn't fall in love, or write a poem'. This may be true, but why not? Is it something to do with emotions? If so, what part do emotions play in intelligence? You might have thought that it's impossible for computers to be creative or respond flexibly to the unexpected. Again, maybe true; but why? Another common answer to this sort of question is that computers are programmed, they obey rules, and these rules are supplied by a programmer. 'The machine is only as intelligent as the program it's given', is the refrain. True. But does it matter? If a machine has an intelligent program then is it important where this came from?

As you can see, the question is a perplexing one.

Artificial intelligence, and particularly its Symbolic AI strand, has suffered a number of powerful attacks. Two names stand out: those of John Searle and Hubert Dreyfus. It would take too much space to sum up the arguments of these two thinkers in detail, but here is a taster.

You may already have heard of Searle's 'Chinese Room' argument, presented in the paper 'Minds, brains and computers' I quoted from earlier (Searle, 1980). For now, I just want to take four points raised by Searle and Dreyfus's critiques and raise them as questions here.

Figure 1.13
Hubert Dreyfus

Figure 1.14
John Searle

1   *Meaning*. I argued earlier that computers are interpreted automatic formal systems. They manipulate symbols that stand for things in the world. But the interpretation of these symbols comes from *us*, from an outside human interpreter. Within the computer, the symbols have only purely formal meaning. For humans, though, intelligence is all about meaning. For a computer, the token 'knife' is simply a pattern of bits, nothing more. But for me, 'knife' has countless meanings, associations and connotations. Moreover, these change according to the *situation* I'm in. 'Knife' has an entirely different meaning for me when I am standing in the kitchen with one, confronting a pot of jam and a slice of bread, than to when I am in the bedroom confronting one in the hand of a jealous lover. How can computers act intelligently when the tokens they juggle have no meaning for them? Haugeland has called this 'the problem of original meaning'.

2   *Rules*. Computers manipulate symbols according to rules. This is a good model of such activities as chess. But are all, or even most, intelligent activities just rule-following? What about medical diagnosis, mathematical problem solving, singing, holding a conversation, writing an Open University course? Can these be summed up in sets of rules?

3   *Representations*. Computer systems depend on a model of the problem or situation they are tackling. This is easy enough in the case of a chess board, since all we have to represent are 64 squares and the positions of up to 32 pieces on them. But most real-world situations are very, very complex. Is it possible practically to represent these as a set of symbols? Can many real-world situations be represented in symbols *at all*?

4   *Intelligence*. Is Symbolic AI dealing with too narrow a conception of intelligence anyway? In choosing activities such as chess and language manipulation as our paradigms of intelligence are we ignoring crucial features of intelligence? Were chess and other board games simply chosen as perfect examples of intelligence *because* they worked well on computers? After all, chess is not just an activity that is easy to model as a formal system – it *is* a formal system.

These questions will come up again in the course, and we'll return to them in Block 6. For the time being, though, just note that even if every one of these doubts is well founded, these are not arguments against artificial intelligence or even against AI. They are arguments against *strong artificial intelligence*. Even if strong artificial intelligence is a doomed project, the construction of limited, but useful and practical, simulations of human intelligence on computers is still a worthwhile endeavour.

6 Conclusion – Symbolic AI and Cybernetics

When I worked in artificial intelligence in the mid-1980s, Cybernetics – if we discussed it at all – was dismissed with a shrug. It was seen as a movement whose time had passed, a rather diffuse set of theoretical pursuits, which had little to show in the way of concrete achievement. Symbolic AI – writing intelligent software for digital computers, based on the principles of representation and search – was the way ahead. AI achieved real results. Cybernetics was just empty theory.

I now think this view was arrogant and quite wrong. But it is true that Cybernetics went into eclipse in the 1960s; AI came to the fore and stayed there. Why exactly this happened is really a matter for historians and sociologists of science. I can think of four possible reasons.

▶ *Multidisciplinarity*. Cybernetics was conceived from the start as a multidisciplinary project, taking in mathematics, computing, engineering, social sciences and the humanities. Although we'd all probably agree that, in theory, this is an excellent approach to such a challenging problem as understanding intelligence and replicating it in machines, it was probably hard to sustain in the research environment of the time.

▶ *Theoretical aims*. Cybernetics' central aim was *understanding*. There was less emphasis on building useful intelligent artefacts. AI promised immediate delivery of working intelligent systems, and produced some impressive and encouraging early results.

▶ *Technology*. The computing technology of the time may have been too weak to be an adequate vehicle for cybernetic systems.

▶ *Competition for funding*. In the 1960s, as now, competition for research funding was intense. There may also have been personal animosity between cyberneticists and Symbolic AI researchers. In 1969 the noted scientists Marvin Minsky and Seymour Papert published *Perceptrons*, a devastating critique of certain computational models of nervous systems, which showed, with unanswerable mathematical arguments, that such models were incapable of doing certain important computations. *Perceptrons* killed most research into neural computing for fifteen years. Much later, Papert confessed in an interview:

> Yes, there was *some* hostility behind the research reported in *Perceptrons* ... part of our drive came ... from the fact that funding and research energy were being dissipated on what still appear to me ... to be misleading attempts to use connectionist methods in practical applications. Money was at stake.

Perhaps most significantly, Symbolic AI and Cybernetics had different starting points. Each began with a quite different view of the nature of intelligence and how it is manifested, and with radically different models. As I noted in the summary earlier, Cybernetics was concerned with feedback, the body in its environment, and purposeful activity; Symbolic AI with digital computation, symbolic representation, rules and abstract thought.

But Cybernetics has not gone away. Indeed it has returned in new guises and under new names. Many theorists now believe that Symbolic AI's indifference to the *body* and to *activity* was (and is) its greatest mistake. Animals (including humans) are *active*: they move around the world, responding to it at every moment. Intelligence is necessary for our never-ending engagement with a complex, dynamic and challenging world. The intelligent mind is not some abstract, remote controller of the body: in every second of life, both mind and body work together to produce useful, purposeful *action*. As you'll see in Block 3, many modern approaches to artificial intelligence, therefore, embrace two new key ideas: *embodiment* (an intelligent system has to have a body) and *situatedness* (this body must interact with, and cope with, a challenging environment, in real time). Since robots fulfil these two criteria perfectly, the future of AI may increasingly belong to robotics. We'll have much to say about robots in Block 3.

7 Summary of Unit 1

You began this unit by taking a quick tour of the Internet, in search of artificial creatures, in myth, fiction and fact. This then became the basis of a wide-ranging discussion – historical, philosophical and technical – of the whole conception of artificial entities, which occupied the rest of the unit.

The discussion fell into four main parts:

1   **Machines**. Here we looked at humankind's age-old dream of artificial creatures possessing some of the powers of animals or even of humanity itself. I posed questions about our attitudes to these – mostly fictional – creations over the ages: were they seen as tools, simulacra, or even something approaching life itself?

2   **Minds**. In this section we considered the possibility of artificial *minds*. I presented some of the historical conceptions of this possibility, particularly the mechanistic model of mind that arose among the thinkers of the European Enlightenment, in which mental operations were perceived as a form of *computation*. I suggested that this model culminated in two twentieth-century intellectual movements: *Cybernetics* and *AI*.

3   **AI**. With the advent of the digital computer after the Second World War there was finally serious interest in the possibility of building machines capable of thought. In this part of the discussion we looked at the birth and intellectual foundations of Symbolic AI and contrasted it with the earlier Cybernetic approach. You also met for the first time the distinction between *strong* and *weak artificial intelligence*.

4   **Computers**. In this more technical section, I presented in some detail the conception of the computer as an *interpreted automatic formal system*. We then moved on to examine two key capabilities of the digital computer: its ability to embody *models* and to solve problems of *optimisation*.

You'll find that these ideas, particularly that of the tension between the Symbolic and Cybernetic conceptions of mind, will underlie the argument of every part of M366.

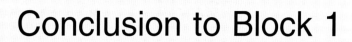

Conclusion to Block 1

Block 1 conclusion

In this block I've tried to take a panoramic tour of an immense landscape of ideas relating to machines, minds and computers. We will take up these ideas in the rest of the course as follows.

In **Block 2** we take a general look at Symbolic AI, the strand in artificial intelligence based on symbolic computation, representation and search – its tools and strategies, successes and failures.

Block 3 investigates the return of ideas from Cybernetics. There we'll question Symbolic AI's focus on abstract activities such as chess and try to frame new definitions of intelligence, taking in the intelligence of animals as well as humans. We develop a new account of how intelligent behaviour can arise – without symbolic models, and without explicit rules – followed by detailed and practical descriptions of working systems based on these new concepts.

Blocks 4 and 5 expand on the ideas developed in Block 3 by describing in detail two projects within artificial intelligence that are based on them. **Block 4** deals with *neural computation*, the original Cybernetic idea of programs modelling the nervous systems of humans and animals, as the key to explaining and replicating intelligent behaviour. **Block 5** investigates *evolutionary computation*, computer systems based on the principles of Darwinian evolution.

In **Block 6**, we return to some of the questions raised in this unit; and you'll be invited to develop your own opinions about the possibility and future of artificial intelligence.

For now, though, look back at the block and unit learning outcomes and check these against what you think you can now do. Return to any section of the block if you need to. You will find further case studies, exercises, links and other supplementary material for this block on the course DVD and course website.

References and further reading

Further reading

Evans, C.R. and Robertson, A.D.J. (eds) (1968) *Cybernetics*, London, Butterworth.

Haugeland, J. (1985) *Artificial Intelligence: The very idea*, Bradford Books, MIT Press.

Winston, P.H. (1992) *Artificial Intelligence*, Bradford Books, MIT Press.

References

Asimov, I. (1950) 'The Evitable Conflict' in *I, Robot*, Voyager (1968).

Cervantes, Miguel de (1615) *Don Quixote*, translated by Ormsby, J., London (1885).

Dean, T., Allen, J. and Aloimonos, Y. (1995) *Artificial Intelligence: Theory and practice*, Redwood City, CA: Benjamin Cummings.

Descartes, R. (1637) *Discourse on the Method*, translated by Veitch, J., London, Dent (1975).

Descartes, R. (1664) *Treatise on Man*, translated by Veitch, J., London, Dent (1975).

Dreyfus, H.L. (1993) *What Computers Still Can't Do: A critique of artificial reason*, Cambridge MA, MIT Press.

Hobbes, T. (1651) *Leviathan*, Oxford Paperbacks (1998).

Hobbes, T. (1656) *Elements of Philosophy Concerning Body*, in *The English Works of Thomas Hobbes of Malmesbury*, Aalen, Scientia (1966).

Homer (2002) *The Iliad*, translated by Johnston, I., Richer Resource Books. Also available at http://www.mala.bc.ca/~johnstoi/homer/iliad_title.htm [accessed 10 August 2006].

McCarthy, J., Minsky, M.L., Rochester, N. and Shannon, C.E. (1955) 'A proposal for the Dartmouth Summer Research Project on Artificial Intelligence' at http://www-formal.stanford.edu/jmc/history/dartmouth/dartmouth.html [accessed 10 August 2006].

Newell, A., Shaw, J.C. and Simon, H.A. (1958) 'Chess playing programs and the problem of complexity', *IBM Journal of Research and Development*, vol. 2, no. 4, pp. 320–35.

Searle, J.R. (1980) 'Minds, brains, and programs', *Behavioral and Brain Sciences*, vol. 3, no. 3, pp. 417–57.

Standage, T. (2002) *The Mechanical Turk: The true story of the chess-playing machine that fooled the world*, Allen Lane.

Turing, A.M. (1950) 'Computing machinery and intelligence', *Mind* (New Series), vol. 59, no. 236 (October 1950), pp. 433–60.

Wiener, N. (1948) *Cybernetics: or Control and communication in the animal and the machine*, Cambridge, MA: MIT Press.

Wiener, N. (1950) *The Human Use of Human Beings: Cybernetics and society*, London, Free Association Books.

Acknowledgements

Grateful acknowledgement is made to the following sources for permission to reproduce material within this course text.

Figures

Figure 1.1(a): Red and white figure volute krater depicting the death of Talos, bronze giant who guarded the Cretan tree painted by the Museo Archeologico, Bari, Italy / The Bridgeman Art Library;

Figure 1.1(b): The Picture Desk Ltd;

Figure 1.3: Mary Evans Picture Library;

Figure 1.4: Science Photo Library;

Figure 1.5: Science Photo Library;

Figure 1.6: Photo © Estate of Francis Bello/Science Photo Library;

Figure 1.7: Mary Evans Picture Library;

Figure 1.8: Science Photo Library;

Figure 1.9: Courtesy of Guray Alsac;

Figure 1.13: Copyright photo: Sijmen Hendriks;

Figure 1.14: Courtesy of John Searle.

Cover image

Image used on the cover and elsewhere: Daniel H. Janzen.

Index for Block 1